#HIGHERSELFIE

#HIGHERSELFIE

WAKE UP YOUR LIFE.
FREE YOUR SOUL.
FIND YOUR TRIBE.

LUCY SHERIDAN
& JO WESTWOOD

HAY HOUSE

Carlsbad, California • New York City • London • Sydney
Johannesburg • Vancouver • Hong Kong • New Delhi

First published and distributed in the United Kingdom by:
Hay House UK Ltd, Astley House, 33 Notting Hill Gate, London W11 3JQ
Tel: +44 (0)20 3675 2450; Fax: +44 (0)20 3675 2451; www.hayhouse.co.uk

Published and distributed in the United States of America by:
Hay House Inc., PO Box 5100, Carlsbad, CA 92018-5100
Tel: (1) 760 431 7695 or (800) 654 5126
Fax: (1) 760 431 6948 or (800) 650 5115; www.hayhouse.com

Published and distributed in Australia by:
Hay House Australia Ltd, 18/36 Ralph St, Alexandria NSW 2015
Tel: (61) 2 9669 4299; Fax: (61) 2 9669 4144; www.hayhouse.com.au

Published and distributed in the Republic of South Africa by:
Hay House SA (Pty) Ltd, PO Box 990, Witkoppen 2068
info@hayhouse.co.za; www.hayhouse.co.za

Published and distributed in India by:
Hay House Publishers India, Muskaan Complex, Plot No.3, B-2,
Vasant Kunj, New Delhi 110 070
Tel: (91) 11 4176 1620; Fax: (91) 11 4176 1630; www.hayhouse.co.in

Distributed in Canada by:
Raincoast Books, 2440 Viking Way, Richmond, B.C. V6V 1N2
Tel: (1) 604 448 7100; Fax: (1) 604 270 7161; www.raincoast.com

A catalogue record for this book is available from the British Library.

ISBN: 978-1-78180-667-8

Interior images: p.255 Sophia Spring; all other photography by Ralph Barklam (model: Ali Marler)

Jo: To Presto, my canine spiritual guru, who chose me for a reason. You are the kindest, gentlest, most unconditionally loving and patient soul ever to walk the Earth. You continue to teach me every day how to accept what is, go at my own pace and love without exceptions. You are always in my heart and the pool is always open, any time you want to dance.

Lucy: To my famalam, Mum, Dad and Oliver, for your encouragement and support always – I chose you well. To Roe, my four-legged goddess, who is my spirit animal in walking and woofing form. And to Alabama, for always letting me be me – even when that means I throw your iPhone and swish my hair around like I own the place (every place!).

CONTENTS

NOTE FROM THE AUTHORS

Hey there hot stuff! Welcome to #HigherSelfie. We're so glad you could join us in this global movement for good. Picking up this book is a great first step if all this spirituality malarkey is new to you. And we hope it will continue to serve as a grounding reminder of core spiritual principles – and their practical applications in everyday life – as you grow into your own spiritual connection. Likewise if you've been meditating for 15 years and are verging on self-professed guru status you'll still find some golden nuggets on universal spiritual themes such as surrender, forgiveness and commitment within our cheeky chapters. After all, however enlightened you are, ultimately we're all still human.

So what are you waiting for? Get inspired to *be* your #HigherSelfie right now – and read on to discover how. Wake up your life. Free your soul. Find your tribe.

Only love,
Jo + Lucy xo

A RALLYING CRY

#HigherSelfie is an unapologetic rallying cry for everyone waking up at this time of spiritual catalyst energy, whether you already identify as being a modern-day lightworker or you're reading this book to figure out what that is.

This is a time on Earth when our intuitive, heart-and-soul-led way of being must become our only way and our challenge is to integrate our social media obsessions, busy schedules and all the other trappings of 21st-century life into that too. Our mission is to help you to navigate the sometimes confusing and overwhelming nature of everything modern life has to throw at you, to your spiritual advantage, so you can become spiritually active in the most empowered way.

SPIRITUAL SMACKDOWNS!

Peppered throughout this book you'll find joyful little nuggets we affectionately call 'Spiritual Smackdowns!' If you've ever met us in person, you'll know that despite the natural pitfalls of being human, we make great efforts be to kind, empathetic, understanding, loving and generous people. That said, sometimes you gotta cut the crap and get straight to the point. Like your big spiritual sisters, who are most definitely on your side 'til the bitter end, we refuse to let you wallow, trip yourself up with sneaky self-sabotage or make paltry excuses that keep you small.

That's because we *know* how awesome you are. If you've picked up this book we're guessing that you're a modern-day lightworker. Whether you're a crystal-wearing, animal intuitive or you drive the night shift on a mail van (or both!), you were drawn to this message, this movement, for a reason.

So, allow us to give it to you straight, for the first of many instances.

We've hit a crisis point on Earth. For too long, we, the human race, have been pillaging finite resources from our beautiful planet for profit. We've been polluting our air and water and food sources, mistreating animals and our environment, and allowing discrimination against minorities, or in the case of women, majorities, for too long. Something has to change. Something is changing.

The tide is turning and this shit no longer flies. The energy of good is rising up.

The collective consciousness is growing stronger. The light is getting brighter. And yes, in response the collective ego is fighting back. We'll talk more about old Mr Ego later, but in case you don't know, that's what it does. When we shine a light on its darkness, it fears its own death and so tries to fight back. It's smart and resourceful because we are. It's a part of us – the collective us. But this rising of the ego is only proof that the light is winning. Ego prefers to have us in state of 'meh' than a state of crisis. In 'meh' we do nothing. We ride along uncomfortably on ego's low-level stream of discontent, ranting at the TV and not much more. In crisis, we act.

To help the light banish the darkness, we need you – turned on, tuned in, shining bright. We cannot afford to have you held back, feeling stuck, hiding or playing small. We need you operating at your full capacity for love and joy, spreading the message of the lightworker, Going out into the world every day and being your #HigherSelfie, however that manifests for you.

So that's why we've included Spiritual Smackdowns, short pieces that pull no punches and give you a quick snap back to the task at hand, to make your life, and therefore the world, a much more amazing place.

INTRODUCING... *A COURSE IN MIRACLES*

In addition to the Spiritual Smackdowns, you'll find it hard to miss the references to *A Course of Miracles* (referred to hereafter as *ACIM*). #HigherSelfie is not a book about *ACIM*, but *ACIM* is a super-important reference point for both of us, and especially Jo, so in case you're not familiar with its teachings here's a wee intro to give you a bit of context for when it pops up.

Jo: *ACIM* – a spiritual path

I discovered *A Course in Miracles* a couple of years ago after a spiritual revelation in my living room. #casual. More than a book. *ACIM* describes itself as psychological mind training and I'm referring to it as an 'it' because no author is attributed to it. Now the next bit might sound a bit woo but stay with me.

Scribed by Helen Schucman, who felt that she was simply writing down the words of an inner, channelled voice that she identified with as being Jesus, *ACIM* uses traditional Christian language but it isn't a religious book and doesn't contain any dogma or doctrine. The point of studying it, as with all spiritual paths, is the attainment of inner peace and it contains the same universal themes that run through all spiritual paths and major religions in their purest forms. So whenever I'm describing it to 'muggles', I say that in principle it's similar to Buddhism as it seems to me that the two paths are closely aligned.

ACIM offers 365 daily meditations, as well as a 'Text' explaining the principles explored through the meditations, a 'Teacher's Manual' and two supplements: 'Psychotherapy: Purpose, Process & Practice' and 'Song of Prayer'. The 'course' doesn't claim to be the best or only spiritual path and nor do we advocate it as such, it's just one that resonates with us. You also don't need to know anything about *ACIM*, or have any interest in ever picking it up, to read and enjoy *#HigherSelfie* – we've done the heavy lifting for you and interpreted the lessons for this digital age.

SPIRITUAL ACTIVISM

There's a cosmic alarm clock going off around the world. More people are waking up more quickly and earlier in life and feeling hungry for inspiration, guidance and community in order to live a bigger, richer, more aligned existence. As the cliché of the midlife crisis alludes to, it was accepted wisdom that if there was going to be an 'OMG!' moment in your life it would likely pop up some time in your 40s or 50s, but increasingly the pivotal point is happening pre-30 and the quarter-life crisis is an actual thing now as a new generation collectively questions a previously unchallenged paradigm. That is, you go to school, play the game, pick a lane and stay in it until the kids have left home and you've retired. You can then finally start to think about and experience the things you've been yearning to – if your mortgage hasn't crippled your will to live by then.

When so many accepted systems and paradigms are changing and being contested by our super-connected millennial generation, we are waking up to alternative ways of living and redefining the rules to suit a more loving and holistic outlook.

The cosmic alarm clock is going off and, finally, we've stopped pressing snooze.

Everyone has their own gateway drug into the 'world of woo' – for Jo it was Gabrielle Bernstein's *Spirit Junkie* and for Lucy it was *The Secret* by Rhonda Byrne. For you it could have been feeling touched by an inspirational post on Facebook, following a blog link to a free meditation or one of many, many different routes in; it may even be this very book, but no matter, the result is the same.

As a global community we are becoming more conscious of how we spend our time and as individuals we are finding our own paths of conscious expression. When Jay Z and Beyonce publicly announce they're trialling a vegan diet, we think we can safely say that conscious living is coming out of the closet and into the mainstream.

But you can't just save your best self for your yoga class or your spiritual Facebook group. It's time to act. If we want to experience the impact of significant spiritual change, not only in the present but also in the ripple effects of future generations, we must participate. While there are still jobs to do, bills to pay and people who need our help, transformation will not grow out of time spent on our meditation pillow or binge-watching motivational YouTube videos alone.

You're reading this book so we're guessing you're at least open to, if haven't yet fully bought in to, the concept of living a conscious life, but we are here to help take your awakening to a new level.

We believe that the people alive at this time on Earth are the catalyst generation.

We each came here to start movements, grow movements, take part, dive in wholeheartedly and act. Act spiritually, emotionally, mentally and, most importantly, physically. All spiritual practice starts within but now it's time to bring it out into the world as well.

We're not suggesting that anyone go around preaching or trying to convince others, not least because all that serves to do is turn people off. Instead we're talking about demonstrating. *ACIM* says 'to teach is to demonstrate,' Gandhi said 'be the change you want see in the world' and your mum said 'less talk, more action'. We need you shining your light out in the real world, in tangible practical ways, as well as in private at your bedroom altar or with your girl gang from nutrition school, who like totes get all this stuff.

We're not calling for evangelism of cultish proportions or for everyone to leave their jobs en masse and join us in a big #HigherSelfie commune (although that would be like the best school camping trip *evah*!) If you're happy being a bus driver or a bartender or climbing the corporate ladder or any other seemingly 'unspiritual' job, that's cool. (Disclaimer: There's no such thing as an 'unspiritual' job, but sometimes they can look and feel that way to our human eyes.) But *it is* time to get creative about how you can shine your light regardless of what your situation is…

You could start a free meditation group at the office, or create a blog documenting your tried-and-true system for transitioning from frantic fast-food junkie to mindful vegan babe. You could start that support group for local refugees that you've been dreaming about in your spare time, or get a group of friends together to volunteer at your local homeless shelter. You could share YouTube videos of your experience with eco-friendly cosmetics to inspire others to try them too. You could create a spiritual book club online or a step-parent support group at a local coffee shop.

There are as many ways to become spiritually active as there are unique people on Earth and we hope we've shown by offering just a few examples that you can start right where you are, use what you've got and begin as soon as you're ready. (PS. Hurry up! We *need* you!)

Weirdos welcome!

You simply can't do your own flavour of spirituality wrong. Welcome to the level playing field where the only rules are the ones you create and the only tactics you need are those of love, surrender, forgiveness and trust, to connect you deeply with Source, so you can work miracles – as you know in your soul you were sent here to do.

You don't have to save up all your spiritual magic for 'when it's appropriate', you can just start sprinkling it around like glitter –

and when you do there's a good chance that others will notice and have an unsolicited opinion (yawn!) on your outlook. But don't worry because their thoughts about your thoughts are really nothing to concern yourself with.

Whether you're waving your conscious colours in the air like you just don't care or not, people will judge you, misinterpret you, assume things and gossip. They may do it to your face, behind your back, over text or on social media, but it's all gravy, because those folks would be doing that anyway. May as well give 'em something good to talk about ;-)

Please know, that from the shock and awe on your parents' faces when you tell them that you're now a professional tarot reader to the mild disdain you get from the girl who was your schoolyard bestie when you talk about your meditation practice, we and thousands like us are moving through the same outside resistance, questioning and frowny faces too, and we absolutely have your back.

Here's the real truth: You are enough as you are right now. Your Spirit is yearning to work through you and your light is ready to pop its collar. Just as the oak tree lives within the acorn, all that potential, strength, beauty and growth is just waiting to burst free from the depths of your heart and be seen and felt by those around you, whether they're ready for it or not.

By being spiritually active you have the power utterly to transform your life for the highest good and all it needs is your open heart and pure intention. Sticks and stones may break your bones but snark can never really hurt you. And yes, we're speaking from experience…

Jo: Reiki for dogs?! FFS!

Back in the day at an old bridge job, I left my *Reiki for Dogs* book out on my desk. I'd taken it into work for a little light lunchtime reading and, though I hadn't mentioned it and only really talked about my spiritual practice and business when asked – which wasn't infrequently – I wasn't hiding it either. Then my boss spotted it and said, 'Oh FFS, Jo! Reiki for dogs!! *Come on!* Is this the thing where there's *no touching?!*' [*Scoff, scoff!*]

All the while my colleagues looked on, awkwardly, almost audibly thinking, 'Oh shit, how's she gonna handle this one?' Deep breath. This is his crap not mine.

'Yes,' I replied. 'It's all in the energy, like those bad vibes I can feel coming across the table right now!' Accompanied by mock body shock from bad vibes and crossed forefingers in the universal sign for 'stay away!' Cue giggles of relief from colleagues and everyone getting on with their day.

Not pleasant to have to handle in the moment but, in the long run, water off the proverbial duck's back. And if it wasn't my *Reiki for Dogs* book, it was my neon pink jacket or my oversized jewellery or big gold iPhone. It was always going to be *something* anyway.

Out-spiriting

There are no agreed metrics of depth or progress with spirituality but ego is not beyond meddling with your practice and connection, so it's not unheard of for a vibe of competitiveness to rear its ugly head in this most divine of ironies on the 'spiritual scene'.

Being out-spirited, that is, being belittled because someone else perceives you to be 'less spiritual' (actual LOL!) – whether it's aimed at your personal high-vibe practice or how you've turned that into a thriving business – is increasingly prevalent. It's kind of gross and so at odds with living in the light.

Entitled attitudes and territorial tendencies are a waste of time and we're very happy to be the ones who call this shit out, if it means stretching each of us to get really spiritually active in the moments when we have the opportunity to go either way. To slime or to sparkle is the choice.

We are each as connected, light-filled and worthy as each other, so whether you've spent thousands attending silent retreats or you're excited to even know there is a self-help section in the bookshop, that connection and truth remain. If you've heard the cosmic alarm clock, we need you active, out there and doing your bit, no experience necessary.

We've been on the receiving end of this sort of cringey behaviour and it's only added fuel to our #HigherSelfie fire. We know we're lucky to be confident enough/thick-skinned enough/have enough of a support system in place to see through it to the truth, so we're calling it out for the sake of every newly awakened spiritual sister and bodhi brother who could otherwise be scared away from an incredible, light-filled, life-changing path because of the false belief that they're not experienced, knowledgeable, initiated or just enough.

A core part of our mission as creators of an even platform where everyone who has something to say can have a voice, is to blow the doors wide open to everyone who's seen the twinkle of a lightworker in their own eyes.

Lucy: Special delivery with love, from your ego xo

At a meeting of spiritual minds I was once lucky enough to be offered the unsolicited opinion, and one given with great self-righteousness, that my work as a life coach meant I wasn't living in the moment enough because part of the work is future vision setting. Yes, the irony of a so-called spiritual person (news flash, we all are!) saying that to me is as hilarious and flabbergasting as it sounds! LOLZ!

Out-spiriting, like all the less desirable aspects of our human natures, only stems from fear and insecurity. It's a special delivery from your ego to keep you disconnected from all that is sacred.

ACIM refers to the ego as a scavenger dog, always looking for scraps of evidence that would prove you are separate. Separate from Spirit, from Source, from everything you hold dear, from everything that is true and from the rest of the world. It would have you feeling like you're a wave separate from the ocean… How terrifying would that be?! A teeny tiny little wave constantly battling and competing with the might of the whole rest of the ocean! #totesscary!

And that is the origin of out-spiriting each other on the burgeoning spiritual scene. It's the ego obsession with separation that drives the need to quantify and qualify what is already innately within every one of us, equally.

With the recent upswell of consciously, switched-on bright young things making the move into professional spirituality old ego is having himself a whale of a time and deploying 'little wave syndrome' all over the place, encouraging us to mark ourselves against one another with our Earthly plane spiritual credentials…

'She's been qualified way longer than me!'

'He hasn't even finished *ACIM* yet?!'

'Ugh! She's already a Reiki Master and I'm only level 2.'

'I've done Ayahuasca… Have you?'

'But can he talk to the animals?'

Don't get us wrong, all the conscious growth, all the striving for greater depth and connection, all the learning and the practice is only taking us in one amazing, awakened, loving direction, but thinking in any way that our work or personal practice makes us better, more spiritual or more enlightened than anyone else, at least temporarily, undoes all the rest of it.

Epiphany envy

Likewise if you've led a relatively calm, even and in the best sense of the word mundane life so far (hey, let's face it, for most of us a good chunk of life is doing the commute, sending e-mails, making dinner and putting the laundry on!) it can be easy to think that you'll never be spiritually 'there' until you've had a stars-falling-out-of-the-sky breakdown moment.

It's true that for many of us it has taken a huge emotional shocker to jolt us awake and make us finally see the light, but it isn't that way for everyone and if it hasn't happened to you yet, good news! It doesn't have to! You can *choose* to have a conscious breakthrough instead of waiting for a breakdown to blindside you. Either way works and you are no less of a mystical unicorn of the Universe if, instead of wallowing in a pit of drug-addled despair for a year before seeing the light, you just 'accidentally' wandered into the mind, body, spirit section of the bookshop and casually picked up your gateway that changed everything during your lunch hour.

Waking up spiritually doesn't require an X-Factor, contestant-style life story to share.

Aside from the fact that it's all relative, as one person's soul-chipping dull ache in a job they're good at but not in love with is another person's gasp-inducing health scare. Whatever it was that woke you up and tuned you in to the cosmic alarm clock it is totally worthy and legit, because there are no mistakes in the Universe.

You are not more or less spiritual based on your moment of awakening.

The moral of the story is, however it happened for you, whatever your epiphany was – even if it looked distinctly un-epiphany-like – thank goodness you're here now.

And if it was a drop-to-your-knees revelation that brought you here, you can choose to transform it into a breakthrough, if you're willing to get conscious around it – there's a reason you were chosen to experience and survive it.

Wherever you're at on your spiritual journey, just remember that life flows on regardless. Lovers leave. Friends drift. Markets crash. Jobs stop working out. Health takes you by surprise.

The spiritual work, whether you're already doing it every damn day or you're new to the scene and on the lookout for some hot tips, won't stop stuff going wonky. It won't stop emotions happening and things hurting. But it will, without fail, give you the peace, clarity and faith to see the difficult days through to the other side and, in time, give you the grace and willingness to learn the lessons that were delivered through the challenges.

It's your cue to take those lemons you've been gifted, whether they felt like a warm fuzzy hug or a killer arse-kicking at the time, and make some delicious lemonade because we're all thirsty.

Don't wait for it, create it

To paraphrase one of our favourite authors, Elizabeth Gilbert, from her book *Big Magic*, ideas and inspiration are alive in the Universe, always looking for a human collaborator.

At the acceptance of your awakening you become a clear channel for the Universe to flow through, and so deliver sonic strength to your spiritual activist potential. This might mean devouring all of your new fave author's books on your Kindle and creating a positive podcast list for your stressed-out boss or attending angel breath workshops. A wealth of avenues is waiting for you to discover them and an abundance of ideas searching for the right human collaborator to bring them to life. And funnily enough that's how #HigherSelfie came to be…

Our friendship began via an exchange of comments on a post in the UK Spirit Junkies Facebook Group – at first glance a seemingly random and inconsequential connection. We started having online catch-ups about life, business, spirituality and everything in between. Somewhere along the way we felt a strong sense that we were supposed to link up in some way. It was a gut feeling with nothing else to back it up, and no immediate opportunities to act on that we could see, so we would just have to hang tough until the Universal penny dropped.

Divine guidance often comes disguised as 'a hunch', a nagging idea that might well seem crazy or totally unfounded, but nevertheless stays with you and is impossible to shake off.

We knew from our very first Skype date that we wanted to do *something* together. We hit it off right away and had stuff in common beyond an obsessive love of dogs (though that is a borderline essential quality in all potential new friends for both of us!) and the fact that we were both doing the spiritual thing outside the growing London scene.

Ultimately there was a feeling that we wanted to create and be part of something much bigger than ourselves. Without being able to articulate it, we both sensed that there was room for something new and fresh in the world of spirituality and self-development. We could both feel the rising tide of, as Ruby Warrington terms it 'Now Age' lightworkers doing their thing, but all in separate, isolated ways – which was kind of a bummer for those of us hungry for the kind of connection that can only come from unifying groups OFF-line. But no matter how much we searched, Googled, exchanged WhatsApp messages and read other people's newsletters – hungry to spot an indication that someone else could scratch our itch – it eluded us. Nobody was displaying an appetite or inclination to tie all the golden strands together.

There didn't seem to be a place offline to gather, grow, share ideas and put our messages out there unless we had already somehow made a big name for ourselves or 'cracked the market' like the few divine doyennes who've come before us.

We could feel that there were modern mystics, holistic healers and spirit-savvy peeps waiting for an opportunity to share their work in a wider way, on a bigger stage than they could leverage for themselves without decades of kudos stacked up behind them, an eye-wateringly high social media following, celebrity clients or some other human metric 'worthy of attention'.

We knew there was no such thing as out-spiriting despite the occasional sliming or incidence of posturing we'd been privy to.

We knew that just because you're not yet a Marianne Williamson or a Robert Holden with decades of spiritual experience (of course it's important to acknowledge that the only thing you need in order to have 'spiritual experience' is air in your lungs) it doesn't mean you don't have something valuable, meaningful and profound to share.

We let the months pass with no idea where this philosophy could manifest in a practical way. We couldn't see it anywhere in our peripheral vision and this is when what Elizabeth Gilbert might term 'Big Magic' began to rise and make its presence known in such a way that was impossible to ignore. Instead of waiting for it, we created it.

The birth of #HigherSelfie

#HigherSelfie was a bit of an ugly duckling at first: an exciting but random and broad bunch of ideas floating around on a big piece of paper with the words 'Punk Your Soul' written in the middle of it. We made the executive decision to give it a crappy working title so we wouldn't get attached to a name or a definition too early. We knew this was going to need some space to reveal itself and its potential.

Still not really sure what the end result would be, we began to nurture this funny-looking bird with weekly status meetings and e-mailed checklists/to dos/updates/more ideas to throw into the melting pot/random Pinterest boards, inspirations or connections, which might just turn our grey-feathered misfit into a beautiful swan. And bit by bit that's just what happened.

We truly believe that the idea of #HigherSelfie was divinely delivered to us, but it took form through the comparatively mundane workings of human activity. Sending e-mails, making phone calls, building websites, getting quotes, creating budgets and ordering water – *lots* of water. All the while feeling ultimate faith that we were on to something, still unclear of exactly what, but making space for the miracle anyway.

On 10 May 2015, with financial backing from our event collaborators, yoga über-brand lululemon athletica, we held our first, and to date, only, spirituality un-conference in a super-cool warehouse in London. The whole idea of an un-conference is that speaker line-up is decided on the day by the audience, who vote for their peers based on what they want to hear most.

An amazing 200 spiritual seekers attended and many posted their talks in our Speaker's Corner to be voted for by their peers on the day. Bookended by our keynote speakers, creator of The Numinous, Ruby Warrington, who Skyped in live from NYC, and our spiritual sister and fellow author, Rebecca Campbell, who joined us IRL, eight members of the tribe graced the stage to share their message. Among them were people who'd been doing 'the work' for years and had tens of thousands of views on their Huff Post blogs, and people for whom this was their very first public speaking gig.

Boys of Yoga provided moving meditations on the mat, while raw chocolate brownies by 100% Natural were munched in our pop-up mall. Our tarot and angel readers were fully booked all day, Celestine Eleven joined us with a fine array of spiritual wares and Erin Petson sold her beautiful zodiac-inspired illustrations.

Positivitea quenched out thirst with their sacred brews and our ethical food truck sold out of vegan gyoza. *And* there was an after party with Aperol Spritz cocktails!

The atmosphere on the day was incredible, the friendships and connections made priceless, and the most incredible opportunities have resulted for our tribe, whether it's a change in career direction, a nudge for a book proposal or simply a wider awakening and increased confidence in their innate spiritual nature.

The biggest compliment we received on the day was from those for whom this was a new experience, who told us that they were nervous that they weren't spiritual enough to attend something like #HigherSelfie, but they felt welcomed and like they belonged. #heartswell

And to answer the question that may or may not have run through your mind but has certainly run though ours, 'Why us? What gave us the right to claim the divine inspiration to start a movement? What makes us so special?'

Precisely nothing.

ACIM says all of the children of God are special and none of the children of God are special, meaning that we are all equally special. None of us is more special, more worthy than another. We are all equally capable of and worthy of receiving divine inspiration. The only difference between any of us is the chutzpah to act on it. To put it more poetically:

The Universe provides the orchard but we must pick the apples.

So if you have a divine calling within you, or can feel a stirring inside, start now. Ignore your hunch at your peril! *Be* the person who would bring your dream to life and *do* the things that would make it happen. Live a passionate, conscious life in whatever way you can and write the pitch. Meditate and talk about your work online. Pray and send that e-mail. Initiate a conversation and engage people in it with you, not so you can lead and dictate, but so you can harness that collective energy for the benefit of all.

And please, don't wait any longer. We need your light. You only have to turn on the news or scroll through your social media feed to see that we desperately need the lightworkers (that's you btw!) to wake up and start doing your work. Your *real* work. We can't afford to wait for you to become a guru on a mountaintop or to finish the illustrations for your oracle deck. We need you now.

I hope that when you read this book, when you see Lucy and I on a stage, when you meet us in person, you'll realize that we are living proof that you don't need to be perfect, you don't need to be an enlightened master, you don't even have to be able to levitate (I know, right?!) to be the person that could change a life, wake up souls or start a movement. You just have to start doing it.

The myth of being ready

And one final note on rocking your light and being a serious spiritual activist: you will never be ready. There will never be a cabin cross-check before your spiritual take-off, or a two-minute warning before the metaphorical storm hits.

Our life in this human suit is short and there's no time for a dress rehearsal before starting your blog, launching your mindful business, going after a life-changing travel adventure or ending the relationship that's dragging you down.

It will always be possible to have more experience, money, advice, motivation and clarity but at what point do you think you'll know you've got enough of those outside-of-yourself qualities to take the leap? The whole point is you won't, because you'll never be as old, wise and experienced as you will be tomorrow, next month, next year. Trust that you'll gain what you need along the way and the act of *doing it* is the only thing that will train you in what you need to keep doing it.

When we launched #HigherSelfie with a one-day event that we felt was special and could potentially be industry game-changing, we were so *not* ready according to the outside world's rhetoric. We were living at opposite ends of the country, didn't know each other all that well, were working several bridge jobs between us, had zero influential contacts, our mailing lists were small and we were still establishing our coaching businesses. All of the things 'they' say you need to go big, we didn't have!

But we decided to do it anyway because we felt a calling and had faith that it came to us for a reason. We simply couldn't wait to acquire the skills and contacts that would make us feel ready to 'do it properly' and guess what? That divine plan that the omnipresent creator, the all-seeing, infinitely abundant, eternally wise and benevolent Universe had in store for us worked out. No shit!

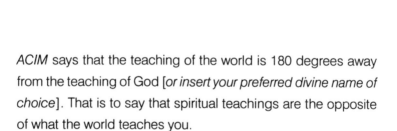

SPIRITUAL SMACKDOWN: IT'S HUMBLE TO KNOW YOUR GREATNESS

ACIM says that the teaching of the world is 180 degrees away from the teaching of God [*or insert your preferred divine name of choice*]. That is to say that spiritual teachings are the opposite of what the world teaches you.

One of the things that the world teaches is that knowing your own awesomeness is arrogant, big-headed and a little bit gross. And yeah, for sure, boastfulness, gloating and generally being ungracious about your wins, whether they're naturally occurring (your easy confidence and wit that can charm the pants off even the starchiest soul at the office party) or they're something you've had to work your arse off for (your recent promotion to

VP, with a PA and a corner office included) is not hot. Nobody wants their nose rubbed in your superiority complex.

But knowing, like really knowing, in your heart and soul as opposed to your ego, your true greatness, is humble, not arrogant. It's humble because it doesn't come *from* you. It comes *through* you. It's humble because this kind of knowing is a sincere acknowledgement that there is something far greater than you at work. It's you demonstrating that yes, you totally bring your own amazing gifts, talents, skills and flavour to the party, but you are not ultimately the Source.

So flip it around and try this on for size. It's actually arrogant *not* to acknowledge your greatness. By not owning the miracle that is you, your life, your purpose and your worth as a channel for the divine, you are saying that the great wisdom that created the intricacies of nature, that every day creates perfect 'coincidences' for you to benefit, learn or grow from, that gives you all the opportunities you could ever need to experience love, gratitude and forgiveness, isn't actually that great.

Or maybe you think you're special, and you're the one they left out, 'Woe is me, the Universe lost my file. It must have done because everyone else's life is soooo perfect and mine isn't. Everyone else gets a break and I don't, boo hoo!' When in truth there is no mistake in the Universe, so if you're experiencing a hard time, it might be an issue of perception, or it might be a lesson you need to learn, but you're not special, and it's not a mistake. It's a gift perfectly designed to help you get to where you really want to be. So instead of fighting your own perfection like you run this joint and make all the decisions around here, relax into it.

Relax into your awesomeness, quietly and gracefully.
Be OK with being much more than just OK, because
of the very fact that you were born. There is
nothing more humble and magnetic than that.

VIBE TALKING

OK, hands up, you got us. We're not quantum physicists. But we're going to go out on a limb here and risk all kinds of Twitter trolling from the wannabe Sheldon Coopers of the world who have a solid grasp of the work of Mr A. Einstein.

For us, the most important 'so what?' of Einstein and his peers' pioneering work in quantum physics can be distilled into an easy-to-grasp truth: that there's a whole lot more going on than any of us can see, hear, smell or touch. Or to articulate it more profoundly, in the words of Jo's coach and one of nature's true wise women, Heather Dominick: 'There is more happening energetically, than not.'

Shivers. Every. Time.

We're pretty sure you know what we're talking about with this expression of so much going on that's unseen. Of all the spiritual principles, this is probably the most universally accepted and understood, even by those who might not label themselves or relate to the term 'spiritual'. But just in case we've lost you down a dark rabbit hole of woo…

+ It's the unspoken spark on a first date that oozes 'I wanna see you again, ASAP!'

+ It's the heavy atmosphere that you could cut with a knife after an argument gets out of hand over text.

+ It's the whiff of guilt and uneasiness when you've been bad-mouthing a colleague behind their back at work.

+ It's the frisson at a really good party when the Spotify playlist is drawing more and more people onto the kitchen dance floor and it's going off!

It's all energy – and it's affecting us, and those around us, all the time.

The stuff we're putting out and the stuff we're letting in. An essential part of creating a really effective spiritual practice is about managing that energy. In fact, if you're looking for one, it's great place to start.

A daily practice

If you want to do it well and enjoy all the crazy cool benefits that come with it, we suggest that energy management becomes part of your daily practice and that you make it work for you and your lifestyle.

Ultimately It will permeate all areas of your life, like reining in that wild ego shit that might have you flying off the handle because your roommate didn't clean the dishes, knowing what to do with the sadness after you see the latest international atrocity on the morning news and learning how to radiate your light so you can go about your day, all killer, no filler, a big fat chunk of the time.

The spiritual path is all nuance, fine lines and grey areas so there is, of course, a caveat – or maybe just an answer to an inevitable question.

When you get told the shiz in the paragraphs above, ego wants to skip right to the nth degree and tell you 'It's not possible to be positive all the time, and isn't that what they're suggesting? Ergo energy management = a load of old phooey. Best just plodding along as you always did, it's kept you alive so far. Plus a *daily* practice sounds *exhausting*.' And, hold the phones, but ego does have something of a point on this one...

Granted, it is impossible to feel 'positive' all the time. We are, after all, flesh and blood. We feel loss and pain. We hurt and grieve. Wounds are opened before they heal and tears flow. Thankfully there's a way to deal with this that is both spiritually aligned and authentic to you. It's all in the energy, of course, and it's possible to *feel sad* but *be* happy at the same time, and we love this parable that beautifully illustrates our point.

There was a monk whose master died. A fellow monk finds him crying by his master's graveside. Implying that one so spiritual should be instantly at peace with his master's death, he asks his brother, 'Why are you crying?'

The monk replies, 'Because I am sad.'

The monk's temporary expression of his sadness doesn't diminish his spiritual connection, nor his overarching happiness, peace and contentment, but in this moment he feels the very human ache of loss.

Feeling anger, sadness, loss or pain doesn't make you less spiritual, but dwelling on difficult emotions doesn't make them, or you, any more profound either.

Consciously feeling so-called negative emotions is not only healthy, it's essential. Just as wallowing in a pit of self-despair is not helpful to you or the rest of the world, neither is being caught in the tyranny of positivity. We need you to be switched on and conscious enough to see, and we mean *really see* what is going on in the world, so you can be aware of where your light is needed. *Contrary to what the Internet tells us, life is not all LOL cats and unicorn farts. Sigh.*

We need you to feel the pain of people who are suffering around the world, without being paralysed by it. We need you to be able to shine your light brightly, without having to ignore the situations and people who need it to do so.

Walking down the street laden with bags after a killer new season haul doesn't feel so great when you see a homeless person asking for change. But you walking around with a dirty chunk of guilt in the pit of your stomach for the rest of the day helps no one. Being inspired to spend some time volunteering at the local soup kitchen or jumping on your iPad to donate the cost of your daily skinny mocha choca latte to a charity that helps homeless people, does.

You can be at peace and feel the full breadth of human emotions at the same time, if you learn how to manage your energy every day. In fact if you take only one thing from this book, let this be it:

> Do whatever it takes every single morning to get yourself into the miraculous space of being a stand-up responsible adult, who shares the authentic light within them and knows how to work it like a boss, saves the drama for her mama, then watches the news, sees the world's prayer list and moves her feet.

Space and flow

Sooo... How do you actually do this magic trick of living life on an even keel most of the time, always able to bring yourself back to a peaceful centre, despite everything modern life, public transport, governments and the Internet has to throw at you?

Our intention is to guide and spark your thinking about what a daily energy practice can be for you, and yet, how you develop and shape it must come from within you.

ACIM says your good intentions are not enough, but your willingness is everything. So to change anything, that is to work or receive a miracle, you must be willing to begin with a right intention. You must be willing to commit to your own spiritual work – which we'll call *the real work* from here on in – every day.

You must be willing to:

+ Try different things and find out what works for you.

+ Build up a toolkit of 'go to' practices that work for you in different situations. (Unless of course you are lucky enough to have a routine you could set your watch to, in which case you probably don't ever have to catch a bus/train/interact with any other humans.)

+ Pick up your practice again, without self-judgement or disparagement, when it inevitably drops.

+ Experience ebb and flow – times when your practice feels profound and times when it feels a bit stale.

+ And you have to be willing to trust that through all of this, if you do it, it will work, and if you don't, it won't.

Before we hit you up with that practical shiz, there is just one more, teensy bit of spiritual concept stuff we need to expand on. The stuff you do on a practical level to help manage your energy is about creating space and flow in your life. Energy needs space to flow. When the space is lacking the flow stops. Here follow a few ways you can create space, flow and an awesome practice:

Free your mind

If there's one conscious living practice that has crept its way into the mainstream it is mindfulness. A widely accessible way to de-stress, we hardly dare whisper its Buddhist origins for fear it will turn the droves of new devotees away! For Lucy in particular, mindfulness has been a great gateway drug to deeper spiritual connection, working in harmony with a regular gratitude practice.

Essentially mindfulness is being really tuned in to what is going on inside and outside us, moment by moment, in gentle compassionate awareness, without judgement. It's a way of noticing what's happening in the physical and emotional realms, including the sensations in our bodies; the sights, tastes, smells and tummy rumbles and, at the same time, being aware of our thoughts and feelings.

In the deadline-centred world, with our experience playing out to the soundtrack of constant social media notifications, it's easy to be completely tuned out of the present moment, looking outside for superficial gratification in a state of overstimulation.

Mindfulness arrests that excess stimulation and soothes the anxiety hangover that comes with it, creating space and allowing us to notice, enjoy and give thanks for life right now. Like the sound of the rain against the window whilst you're tucked up inside, the smell of delicious food as you walk past your favourite pizza joint (mmm piiizzaaa!) or the way the light from the dancing candle flame creates a silhouette of your lover's face against the wall. This is the exquisite detail of life available to us in each moment, which can easily be missed in the rush and push of the autopilot approach to our precious time on this planet.

To really break down the concept like the Beastie Boys break beats, we literally have nothing without our next breath. For a quick, simple, try-anywhere mindfulness hack, close your eyes, or lower your gaze if you're in public, and turn your whole focus on to your breath. In and out. Slow and steady. Calm, peaceful, profound giver of life. Moment by moment, there is nothing else without this.

Don't hate, meditate!

Anyone can meditate. It's a word used a lot in spiritual circles but there's confusion over what it is and how to do it. We like the dictionary definition for its accuracy as well as its accessibility: 'To focus one's mind for a period of time.'

Note, this is not just about sitting down and relaxing… Chilling on the sofa watching Netflix sadly does not count as meditation. Meditation is a way of pressing the reset button on your mental, emotional and spiritual systems. It cleanses your thoughts and literally rewires your brain. As with all good practices, the effects are cumulative, so the more consecutive days you meditate, the stronger and more consistently you, and everyone you come into contact with, will feel the effects. Meditation centres and grounds you. It aligns you with a deep inner sense of peace and helps you see the truth through the drama, and experience calm and patience instead of the fraught-ness that modern life inspires. And it doesn't need to take very long either. Bonus!

There are many different practices, techniques and styles – you only need to do a quick Google to discover all the different flavours of getting quiet and going within. Just off the top of our heads there's yoga, if moving meditations are your thing, mindfulness as we've mentioned, Zen meditation with its roots in Buddhism, often practised seated in the half-lotus position, Mantra or OM Meditation where a word or phrase is chanted to focus the mind on a desired intention, then there's transcendental meditation, which is an art of its own taught by certified teachers and practised for 15–20 minutes twice per day.

A common myth about meditation is that it's all about emptying your mind, which can be scary and off-putting for some people – we get it, it ain't easy in this age of overwhelm!

Jo: Getting into the zone

For me meditation isn't about trying to empty my mind or banish 'irrelevant', 'negative' or 'non-constructive' thoughts, not least because I believe that all the thoughts that come into my head do so for a reason, but more on that in a moment. Meditation is a time for my top-quality thoughts. It's when I get into the zone of my highest vibes and, if I'm experiencing a difficult situation, I use that energy to unpick, with love, exactly what needs to be done. Meditation for me is also a time when I make myself available for über inspiration. If ever I'm going to channel a killer idea, or finally work out the missing piece to a life jigsaw I've been working on for ages, it'll be during or right after meditation.

And a final tip from moi. I use the 'wave technique' to deal or not deal with, as the case may be, uninvited thoughts during my meditation time. When a random thought pops into my head like 'Hmmm… What to have for lunch today?' I just let it wash over my brain like a wave gently crashes on the shore and let it wash back out again, trusting that as quickly and easily as it came, it can leave too. No judgement, just acceptance, love and letting go.

If not having to try and empty your mind to meditate appeals, we personally enjoy guided meditations, which do exactly what they say on the tin. You simply tune in to a voice that guides you through a visualization of some sort, whether it's a walk through a landscape, cocooning yourself in protective golden light or sending high vibes to an awkward relationship. You can buy them on iTunes, stream them on Spotify, look them up for free on YouTube or, listen to a special #HigherSelfie meditation which you can find at higherselfie.co/giftmeditation

And then there are the daily meditations from *ACIM*: daily explorations that build on the concepts taught over the period of the course are very instructive and tell you what to think about, exactly how much time to spend and how often to do them.

Whatever form you choose *ACIM* says that five minutes spent with Spirit in the morning means it's in charge of your thought forms for the rest of the day. We reckon that's a pretty good return on investment, no? If you don't believe us, try it. It might just change your life ;-)

Pray

Aaaah! Scary religious sounding word! Come back, come back, it's only as religious as you want it to be – including not at all!

Think of it this way; if meditation is a time to listen – a time to receive the divine light and inspiration of the Universe, a precious focused space in which to hang out on higher planes of consciousness, whether on your own or with your angels and guides, and soak in all the wisdom and abundance Big U has to offer – that makes prayer a time to ask. We use the word 'pray' simply because it sounds poetic, but if that doesn't work for you, as always, just switch it up! So with that clear, we'll continue to use the word pray, if that's cool with you babe?

It's important to pray because you have free will. That means the Universe will not come into your head at night and take away all your dodgy, difficult or destructive thoughts. That would be theft. After all, your mind is your own to do with as you wish. Prayer, however, is your opportunity to ask for help and hand over any crap you're struggling with. Like the perfect combination of the CEO who knows exactly what to do and the assistant who is just waiting on your call, the Universe merely needs you to ask in order to do its thang.

ACIM says that your problem is not that you ask for too much but that you ask for too little. The Universe is eternally, infinitely abundant. That concept is super-hard for tiny human minds to grasp because everything we encounter in this life, aside from our Spirit #natch, is finite. But trust us – as above, so below – infinite means it can never run out. There is always enough. There is always more than enough. So you can't ask of the Universe too often. Ask in your head, out loud or on paper. Ask for stuff you can't handle on your own to be taken away and ask for whatever you're working with to be transformed for your highest good. Just don't ask for a list of specifics. The Big U is not your errand boy. If you knew what the best outcome would be, you'd be there already, right? So accept that we all need some help and let the heavens handle it.

Creating space and keeping it clean

It's important to recognize that living a peaceful life, a life where you can effectively manage your energy and get back to centre even when the world does its absolute best to throw you off, is living a balanced life. Yes, floating serenely on a pillow in a fog of incense will massively up your meditation game, but when the rent is due that ain't gonna help you. So, while the final piece of the energy jigsaw might seem pretty mundane, it's an essential part of any energy practice. Welcome to being human! Ready for your homework? It's time to clean up!

Clean up – emotionally, spiritually, financially

Apologies you haven't said, meditations you've missed, bills you haven't paid. Clean that shit up. It's psychic weight you don't need. Life throws us enough curveballs without having to lug the bulk of avoidance around with us. Got a debt you can't afford? Set up a payment plan. Got someone in your life you're struggling to forgive? Meditate and pray on it. Can't make time for your spiritual practice? You do pee, right?

Clean up – your home, your car, your wardrobe

Ever heard the distinctly un-profound, but oh-so-true saying, 'Messy bed, messy head?' In our spiritual practice, if the surroundings are a shit show, it's a lot more likely that our thoughts and actions will be too.

It's much easier to focus and, y'know, find stuff when the physical space you inhabit is clean and tidy. There's a school of thought that says if you clean your house first, then get busy doing the work of your calling, you're telling the Universe that you value doing chores over what you really love. We say hooey! The Universe knows what you love and value. The Universe knows that spending some time de-cluttering the under-the-stairs cupboard (yes, that hell hole!) and mopping your floor doesn't mean you want to be a professional cleaner (unless, of course, you do, in which case it knows that too!). We don't really need to tell the Universe anything, except that we respect, cherish and are grateful for our piece of the garden. We clean our bodies every day with soap. We clean our minds every day with meditation. We need to remember to clean our material possessions too. It's only right to treat well *all* the gifts you were given, and doesn't the lightness of more space, less dirt and one less thing 'to do' feel soooo good?!

Clean up – your schedule, your to-do list

In the 'busy as standard' pace of modern life with offline commitments and online distractions all vying for our time and attention, it has never been more important to take a breath and review how we use our time. Cleaning up your diary can be a truly expansive and de-stressing exercise that signals to the Big U that we are not sleepwalking through our human excursion to Earth.

So check your schedule for over-scheduling. See where you're pushed to the limit for time and energy. Be especially keen with this on 'social' activities. For example if you find your yoga class at 9 p.m. exhausting and throwing your digestive system into disarray, find one better suited to your timescale. 'Obligatory' after-work Friday drinks leaving you feeling drained and too hungover, too often? Make it every other week, or suggest dinner instead. Competing with yourself (and secretly your colleagues!) to get into the office early every day even though it's killing you and you're spending your whole salary on fancy cream to combat those dark circles? Flex your flexi-time, giirrrllll! If you know a 10 a.m. start suits you best, own it!

A FOMO-motivated 'yes' to too many invitations, then suffering from the anxiety that comes with being permanently on the go? Try the rule of three. Do three things, really well, every day. Anything else is a bonus. Example: Do your spiritual practice really well. Do your work really well. Do a delish dinner with your boyfriend/girlfriend/housemates/mum and dad really well. Congratulations. You had a great day and the people around you really got to enjoy being with you.

Apply the same rule to your to-do list. Try dramatically reducing the amount of stuff you're trying to fit into every day. Get real about how much time it takes actually to do something well. Keep a 'someday/maybe' journal for wild, exciting, not-top-of-the-pile ideas. If and when it's important enough it will naturally make its way on to the real to-do.

When you free up the energy to be present and shine your light brightly you're much more likely to have 'Book round the world flights for sabbatical trip' at the top of your to-do, on an otherwise average Tuesday.

There's an African proverb that says, 'When you pray, move your feet.' In the modern world clearing clutter, paying overdue bills and stopping your over-scheduling habit is one awesome way of moving your fabulous feet. So lace up your hot new high tops and get a wiggle on, babe!

SPIRITUAL SMACKDOWN: ENERGY VAMPIRE VS. MARTYR

Once upon a time there was an awesome young woman who had worked really hard to get her shit together. She was climbing the career ladder, playing the dating game and having fun (with a few hilarious anecdote-worthy nights along the way). She had her own place in a city she loved and rocked her style like Carrie Bradshaw in her early noughties heyday.

But, (there's always a but) she had this one friend, or should we say 'friend', who was a total drain. Lovely girl, just a little too caught up in her own drama, of which there was a lot. She'd guilt-trip our gal into over-scheduling because she didn't want to spend the night alone. She'd call our gal after a killer day at the office spouting her cheap drama down the phone, without so much as a forethought or a 'Hi, how are ya?' She'd constantly compare herself to our gal, out loud, sharing (ain't always caring!) how woeful her own life was and how amazing it must be just to 'have it all' like our babe. Not to mention the seemingly unfiltered shit reel she chose to share with the world on social media. Our gal dreaded the notifications coming through, but couldn't seem to do anything about it. After all, they were friends, and a friend in need is a friend indeed, right?!

If this modern fairy tale sounds familiar then you might have what is a little ruthlessly termed an 'energy vampire' (harsh but true!) on your hands.

The truth is, if you have a 'friend' like our fictional protagonist does, you may be suffering from a severe lack of boundaries in your life, and that ain't serving no one, not you and definitely not your pet vampire, and here's why… There's a pretty distinct line between being compassionate and being a martyr. The bitter irony is, in your desperate need to be nice and supportive and an unending pit of tea and sympathy at any time of day or night, you're actually helping your friend to stay stuck, or as those with many letters after their names and 'therapist' on their business card call it, 'enabling'.

It's hard when you love someone but sometimes you've got to let them feel their own pain, make their own mistakes and figure it out for themselves. No one learned to ride a bike without falling off a few times, so stop being their metaphorical training wheels, because quite frankly you're holding them back.

Friends like this don't need you to hold their hand, as much as they might protest that they do. What they really need is for you to hold space. (Ding ding ding! Ten points in Woo Woo Bingo for that phrase right there!) But what does that mean? It means you're the friend who doesn't buy into their drama with them. You're more convinced by their capabilities than their catastrophes and you mentally, spiritually and practically, if you can, hold space for their true self to emerge.

And if you recognize yourself in the vampire, (and truly, no judgement, we've all been the needy one!) check yourself before you wreck yourself. You got this, sister, and you can totes handle whatever life hands you today. But if you really feel like you can't... Congratulations, you're in the right place – just read on and let us give you a metaphysical leg up.

EGO COAT CHECK

There's a lot of talk in the world of woo about this thing called the 'ego'. We're not talking about the same thing as the Freudian-derived ego (or more accurately a killer combo of Freud's id and super ego), where we accuse someone of having 'a big ego' as an umbrella term for their posturing or need to be the best and be loudly acknowledged as such.

Certainly the ego we speak of can influence you to act in that way, and is also a scavenger that will use any scrap of evidence it can find to help you self-sabotage the good feelings and experiences you're having, by whatever means it can.

The ego we're speaking about is more concerned with littleness; with keeping you small, under the pretence of keeping you 'safe'. The ego as in the little blighter *ACIM* speaks of is your false self – the part of you that has you self-sabotaging at every turn.

Put into context, this is how it operates. Let's imagine for explanation's sake you're on a wellness kick. It's going really well, you've downloaded the fitness app your BFF recommended, the fridge is full of dark leafy greens (fangirling over kale anyone?!) and you've cut down on the vodka tonics at after-work drinks. You're feeling good and the results you wanted are happening. Then sometime on an idle Tuesday the immense desire for a sticky ooey gooey doughnut kicks in. Did we also mention that you're allergic to gluten and off sugar? But you can't help it. Krispy Kreme is calling and the urge is strong. Ego can sniff this self-sabotaging desire like a fart in an elevator and immediately kicks into action.

'Go on treat yourself, you've been doing so well, while helping you to push way back in your mind how bloated and gross you'll feel afterwards. So off you go to the doughnut shop and you fill your face with glee, and (enter ego, stage left) almost instantly feel bad afterwards.

Even though you're standing there looking gorge in your new galaxy print leggings, you've dropped your own commitment to healthy eating, and you're about to feel super-uncomfortable for the rest of the day. Then ego, yeah, the same one that lead you astray then guilt-tripped you for the decision, now has a great idea... Well you've busted your resolve anyway, so why not have another doughnut? The pretty sprinkles will make you feel better... And on and on! You know it, right? That total crazy maker that lives inside your head?!

The ego is the part of you that takes on the stories of your past and plays them back to you whenever you want to move forward.

It keeps your stuck in your comfort zone – or your uncomfort zone as it should perhaps be known – and takes any opportunity to help you miss, twist or self-sabotage opportunities and miracles that the Universe has sent for you.

> The ego does not have morals, nor is it discerning. It is smart because you are and is just as adept at puffing you up and giving you a superiority complex as it is at dragging you down when you are on a high.

Jealous pangs triggered by a friend's awesome press interview that you see on Instagram, even though you just landed the client of your dreams? Ego.

Judging someone in your industry as a fake and undeserving because you feel they're getting ahead of themselves and don't deserve the success? Ego.

Smug as f*ck that you've lost 20lbs and all the clean eating has made you look waaay better in that dress that your sister also has? Ego.

Now on the downward spiral because your best mate is doing the same program and is even more ripped than you? Ego.

It knows exactly what would be needed at any moment to bring you back to small and safe and take you away from lit up and expansive, and it has a field day on social media with a never-ending stream of content for it to grasp at and use against your true sense of self. And it's important to note: the ego is not above turning your spiritual practice against you. Many a time we've seen (and experienced first-hand) how the ego can cleverly turn a 'sign from the Universe' into a great excuse not to take that fantastic opportunity, or make meditation into procrastination or commitment into a soul-crushing obsession.

Lucy: No, with love

The need to fit in and be liked has been a recurring theme in my life, until recently, which is kind of ironic because I've always identified with a punk kind of energy. For me, my ego has told me it's unspiritual to say 'no' or set boundaries with people, and I've had to work at this consciously to break out of the constricted, tight space it keeps me in.

In reality, on our spinning planet, some people will take the piss out of you, are on the make at all costs, and are happy to dominate you and your dreams and bring a heap of funky energy into your life bubble if you let them. When people showed this behaviour, my ego sold me the line 'That's just who they are and it's unspiritual for you to criticize or object because that's not conscious living is it, Lucy?' But ego was preventing me from standing in my power, being heard and making the impact I'm supposed to in this lifetime.

How can I fill everyone else's cosmic cup if mine is as empty as my ego would have it? How can I expand, challenge and create a bigger, better version of myself, if I don't have the time and space to work on that? So now I choose to say no, with love. I push back on timings that don't work for me and I'll recommend an alternative if a suggestion doesn't feel like a fit. In doing so, I'm protecting my energy and living super-consciously, standing in my power. Even if the result is a bit of gossip getting back to me about 'my super-busy schedule'. My ego may not be cool with that, but I am.

There are as many theories on how to deal with the ego as there are techniques for tapping into your own lightworker capabilities, and we are big believers in doing whatever works for you, but our ego coat check analogy is a deliberate one. Your ego is like a biker jacket, not a deliciously soft nappa number that moulds to your physique, rather one from the reject bin, with the studs on the inside. Ouchy!

> You have the choice to check your ego at the door, because you don't need it, it doesn't serve you and it definitely doesn't look cool.

For us the ego, AKA the shadow or monkey mind, is something simply to be accepted. By virtue of our human nature, free will and crazy modern world, the ego is within us and can be triggered at any moment, especially if we are spiritually undisciplined. It's just there. If we think of it as darkness, the only way to get rid of it is to shine light on it.

You cannot fight darkness. You cannot swing a baseball bat at it and make it go away. You can't unfollow it on Facebook or delete its number. You can only turn on the light. So through meditation, prayer and conversation with our angels, we can turn on the light that shines away the darkness of the ego. The more practised we get at shining our light, the weaker the darkness gets; the less able it is to overcome our light at unexpected moments.

Practice comes with keeping an eye on it and being an observer of your thoughts like a blogger might capture a fashion show. We're not suggesting you live-Tweet what's in your head – but hey, whatever works! We're simply saying be mindful of the words, interactions and energies that are coming from your ego rather than your intuitive, authentic self. And when they crop up, send love by using the light force – write a comment of congrats on Facebook on your mate's engagement announcement post, even though you're not exactly a fan of her fiancé. Call a truce on that silent grudge with the girl at work. Text that guy to apologize for ignoring his messages on Tinder, if you know you were being Queen Snark and he was just trying to be nice.

As we train our minds, thoughts and actions to dwell in light, they become less vulnerable to the ego's wily ways. The light can be switched on at any moment, and is no less effective if you haven't used it for a while, but the benefits are cumulative if worked regularly.

Whenever ego takes hold, whether you can see it coming, are in the midst of an ego-induced slump or are clambering dazed and confused out the other side of a recent bout of ego overdrive, your awareness is everything. The moment you become aware of what is happening you can flick your light on faster than you can say 'uncomfort zone' and get back to a healthier equilibrium.

So be active and conscious and check your ego at the door because that truly is a giant leap in itself and we have a feeling it will be popping up again along the way – in this book and, y'know, in life.

PALMS OPEN, FINGERS CROSSED. WE SURRENDER!

Whenever you hear about surrender outside of a 'woo woo' context it brings to mind battlefields or war zones, where forcing, planning and strategizing, ensued by fighting, destruction and desperate situations are brought to a close by the submission, voluntary or otherwise, of one of the parties involved. Heavy, man!

But in spiritual terms surrender is not to do with pushing or forcing, manipulating or controlling. Nor is it to do with giving up, giving in and doing nothing. The thing is, surrender is actually one of the most active, conscious practices you can start, and when done consistently it will help you to become truly aligned with your #HigherSelfie and create the conditions for what you desire and deserve to come into your life.

Lucy: Chicken with (un)holy basil

I once pretended I liked Thai food (I don't) just so I would impress a guy who said he wanted to explore South East Asia. In my head, by controlling how he perceived me he'd soon realize we were a perfect couple and, as we'd been on, like, three dates I wanted to close this deal! I can't even remember his name now.

That's just one example of how I used to be a total control freak, messing and meddling in almost everything, from the wording of an e-mail to someone else's holiday plans. WTF?! At best this was irritating for those around me and at worst it was a consistent and effective saga of self-sabotage. Surrender. Changed. Everything.

But the rub is, 'surrender' gets a really bad press. I recently asked some girlfriends what sprung to mind when I said the word 'surrender' and what I got back was…

'Desperation.'

'Retreat.'

'Failure.'

'Surrounded, with no way out.'

'Giving up.'

'Abandoning.'

There was a time when I would have nodded along to those descriptions too. I mean, who wants to throw in the towel? Who wants to give it up and not go the distance? Or worse, be vulnerable to attack?

To surrender is the most symbolic demonstration to the Big U that you're making room for signs, miracles and abundance, and often a mega hat-trick of all three.

Why does it feel so hard to surrender sometimes? Where do we allow resistance or doubt to creep in and throw us off the surrender pony?

In the West we're brought up to believe that assertive energies, including controlling language and forceful tactics, are prized as best, or even the only, practice when it comes to achievement. Chest-beating optional.

How often have you been in a lecture, meeting or just a casual Sunday afternoon convo with your parents or mates and, in the context of talking about your goals, you've been told to:

+ 'Study *hard*.'

+ '*Make it* happen.'

+ '*Fight* for what you deserve.'

+ '*Give it everything* you've got.'

+ '*Push* harder.'

+ '*Take* the bull by the horns.'

+ '*Force* the hand of others.'

- ✦ 'Stay in *control*.'

- ✦ '*Keep on top* of the competition.'

And on and on…

Anyone else starting to feel their heart beat faster while a tense energy creeps into their stomach and their shoulders hunch up as if they're bracing themselves for something… Like a fight?!

But all too often, despite the anxiety-inducing tone, these controlling, forceful energies show up to run things in our lives, under the false belief that this is 'just what it's like' or 'how it's done.'

Think about moving house or looking for that new apartment rental. We're told that it's going to be a rough ride, nice places are scarce and are gone as soon as you've Googled them, getting a deposit together is murder, landlords are crooks and you have to be on your guard because that's just the way it is! The result is we end up pissed off, on the defensive and in a spin, caught somewhere between being on a power trip (got it all handled, bitches!) and being powerless (I have absolutely nothing handled, Mum!!), as we try to control all the odds.

The whole concept of surrender feels scary because we're taught that openness = vulnerable and vulnerability = bad.

I mean, who in their right mind hands over something as essential as where they're going to live to 'the Universe'?!

No wonder surrender feels reckless or like it's a cop-out if it's perceived as the opposite to 'getting shit done'. Opposite approach to success must mean opposite results to success, right?

Um, wrong!

At this time on Earth, with divine feminine energies rising, the old guard of push and force, take and make is starting to feel out-dated and inauthentic. Worse still, it pulls us off our connected faith-full game and out of alignment with the deep wisdom inside of us.

Surrender gets a makeover

We lightworkers need an alternative manual for going about life. As part of a big collective 'no thanks' to a controlling, forceful use of energy, we get to choose consciously our own approach to creation in our lives. Thankfully, it has nothing to do with groping a bull's horns. Whoever came up with that bat shit crazy idea anyway?!

The alternative is the act of releasing the handbrake on abundance – that is the need to control – and letting life-force energy (as opposed to ego energy) do its thing to guide you, through its own perfect motion, to your divinely reserved place of happiness and greatness.

Surrendering sends out a flare that you're open to the potential of what the present moment holds, whether that's making badass spiritual moves or being the willing vessel for receiving.

An important thing to know about surrender is that what you get delivered may not always be the perfect Pinterest-worthy outcome you were dreaming of. There may be more of a process involved and the relevant next step might be a hard-hitting lesson, but trust that whatever happens will be exactly what you need to help you become the person you need to be, to have all that you desire *and* that it's already waiting for you.

Try this. Clench your fist hard. (Not the one holding the book!) How much space is there between the tight fold of your bloodless little finger? Hardly any – I'm guessing you'd struggle to get a teaspoon of pink glitter in that space, forget the shit ton of miracles you've been waiting on. In this instance, if your fist is your life, those tiny cracks and gaps are the metaphorical space available to you when you resist surrender.

Now hold out your hands and raise your palms to face the sky and see the space you've created. There are no sides or a top to the potential of the space. If you were to pour pink glitter (what else?) on to that surface there would be so much space it would overflow! There would be no limit to the amount of pink glitter (read abundance and awesomeness) that you could receive into your amazing new open-armed, open-palmed life. That's what it looks and feels like to live in a state of surrender.

'Open-palmed' is a phrase commonly used at #HigherSelfie HQ, especially when we have a big idea or a dream-level goal that our ego mind would tell us we're 'not ready for', 'is unrealistic' or ask that killer-dream-crushing question 'Who are you to…?'

Every day in this job that doesn't feel like a job running #HigherSelfie, putting the theory of open-palmed surrender into practice is a necessary requirement, not a 'nice to have'. A bit like a dentist needs a reclining chair to do her job properly, we need surrender.

Sometimes we even sit in meetings with our hands facing palms up like we're about to catch a ball, in a physical pose of surrender, because we really want the Big U, as well as our colleagues, investors and clients around the table to *see* surrender in how we hold ourselves as clearly as we *feel* it in our souls.

'Open palms' have called clarity, peace and abundance in for us, and it will do the same for you when coupled with an intention to stand back and let spirit work its high vibe magic.

'But Lucy, Jo, what if it's something I *reeeealllly* want?' Well in that case you may use our (patent pending) fingers crossed, palms open technique. Try it! Cross those lucky fingers but keep your palms open. That's woo-woo sign language to the heavens for 'This means the world to me and feels really frickin' right, but I surrender and trust that you have the master plan. I'm so ready for this or something better!'

Hand it over

Making surrender a way of life is an ongoing thing and we're practising it every day as we hope you're open to (see what we did there!) and our BFF Louise Androlia has been a wonderful role model.

Lou will not get out of bed in the morning without exclaiming 'I surrender!' out loud with her head still on the pillow – goodness knows what her LA neighbours think of that – they're probably, like, totally inspired – but who cares anyhoo? It works for her and it keeps her conscious, grounded and committed to creating the space for possibility and intuition to lead.

What Lou knows is that surrender is not a form of abandoning something, or living in not-so-blissful-ignorance. (We'll bet your Monday morning serenity would be shattered if you 'abandoned' paying your rent – 'The Universe has my back, man!' – and awoke to the sound of the eviction notice being pinned to your door!) It's a very conscious act of handing it over. All of it.

Think of it like having VIP privileges where you get to defer and delegate to a higher power, with a more able and willing miracle department than your human suit could ever have on its own, and it asks for nothing in return other than you trust that the Universe is in charge and has your best interests at heart for the highest good. If you want to go to the advanced level you can start practising just *being* surrendered all the time. That way you won't have to ride the emotional roller coaster by handing stuff over when the shit hits the fan, and grappling it back when it's smooth sailing again.

Jo: Getting down and staying down

I once heard one of the most consistent spiritual voices in my head, Marianne Williamson, tell the story of the moment she realized that it was exhausting getting down on her knees to pray for help and surrender every time shit got real, then hauling herself back up again when she thought everything was OK and she could take it from here, thank you. She just figured one day 'Marianne, why don't you just stay down there?'

For us, handing it over and staying in full faith means finishing off our prayers, desires, aspirations and thoughts closely with the mantra: 'This or something better'.

As far as the Universal energy of love is concerned it's actually impossible for you to miss out once you've asked. It will free you from the human constructs you've projected, or the Pinterest mood board you've been obsessing over! As we hope you've realized by now, you're pretty damn amazing as you are, but the Universe has the added bonus of not being held back by past experiences, future trips or what your mates are up to on social media.

Your prescription prevents perfection

We must get clear on this once and for all. You simply cannot imagine or conceive the greatness that life wants you to experience every single day. Universal abundance is infinite, but that can be pretty hard for us to get our human brains around, as powerful as they are. That means that greatness and wonder are not just reserved for birthdays or holidays or when you've busted a new move at the gym.

It's easy to lie awake at night letting your thoughts, feelings and energy whirl obsessively around a specific person or situation. It's exhausting to be home to the nervous and draining energy of expectation and uncertainty, borrowing a helluva load of drama from the future in the hope you might manifest something exactly the way you want it. Or rather exactly the way you *think* you want it. Again, the Universe has probs got something way bigger, cooler and more kickass in store for you, if only you'd stop wearing the Captain's hat!

Even in an awakened state we can fall foul of our ego's grip, where our rational mind interferes with divine laws to design and prescribe, how, when and what will show up for us.

Lucy: Once upon a bridge job

Jo and I have had many bridge jobs in the past to help us to transition to our full-time light work and our friendship has seen us having to rally each other on countless occasions when the will just to get there, and the reality of where we were, brought us to an ugly, snot-bubbling cry! Sometimes we took turns and other times it was a mutual bawling sesh!

One of Jo's bridge jobs was poorly paid, had long hours, was physically, emotionally and mentally exhausting, and started to take its toll outside of her challenging shift rota. She prayed for a miracle and as she's my BFF I did my part to support her to find a new position with the very lowly brief of 'it should not be shit, thank you very much!'

Roll on a couple of months and Jo applies for a great position at a really cool company, gets an interview, hits it off with the team, gets a second interview and although she totes doesn't expect it (and neither do many folks close to her – she's got a wild CV, that one!), she lands the role.

Amazing, yeah? Double back flips, right? Naked streaking down the corridor, surely? Weellll, not immediately, no. It was more a case of the 'I'm not sures' and 'yeah buts'.

Ego had stepped in to try and convince Jo that this better paid, more flexible, kinder and easier in many ways job was maybe not the right move. She (read her ego) was concerned that she was being tied into a contract... What if something big happened with #HigherSelfie and she needed to be outta there, or she needed more flexibility, or there was a meeting she absolutely had to be at no matter what because it was a one-time opportunity only?!

The Universe had only delivered everything she had asked for and more, and so the ego naturally feared its own death. So it got to work concocting all kinds of reasons why she'd be better off staying in her current situation, and it almost had her for a minute there.

Needless to say, we talked it over and she saw the light! Jo realized that not only did she need to surrender to the ask for a better situation, but also to trusting that what had appeared, seemingly out of the blue, would be the perfect divinely delivered solution – otherwise why else was this really cool opportunity right in front of her? She handed her notice in the following Monday and soon got to work at her final and much better-suited bridge job. Her surrendered state delivered big time.

We know a higher power is always waiting to be asked to scoop us up but we can often be slow to take advantage of it because of the belief that we only have our own strength to rely on. If you've thought about it, you want it, you've asked for it and stepped back, then it's surrendered. Consider it handed over to the most powerful forces of creation – how's *that* for a concierge service?!

Your next job is to play your part and meet your dream halfway. For example, getting that ideal job will require you to leave enough time to complete a knockout application form. Being debt-free will mean you call the bank and get clear on how you'll pay off your credit cards. Reconnecting with the friend you fell out with might mean a phone call or 'how are you?' text so you can apologize for your part in the fight.

It's important to be accountable to the end result and yet it's not for you to engineer every part of it. Be ready to meet the miracles halfway and accept that the outcomes are for the highest good. Again, if you have all the forces of creation conspiring to gift you happiness beyond what your human mind can conceive, you need to be OK with it maybe coming in a different-coloured box to the one you think you ordered.

Either the Universe is in charge or it's not

Nobody has a special arrangement with the Big U, which means only certain things are surrendered. Like 'OK God, you can have my relationship, my career and my money… but I'm holding on to my diet and fitness because when it comes to my body I have to have control of what I eat and how I move down here on Earth and what do *you* know about that?! If I'm gonna lose all this weight then it's going to need *my* focus, but y'know, you can have the rest of it.'

Ahem!

> **Either the Universe is in charge or it's not! Either you can put your trust and faith in the all-knowing power and wisdom of the Universe, that little old thing that rules the solar system, makes the rainforests grow, rivers flow and tides move. Or you can handle it. Whatever.**

That's why surrender as a conscious state of existence is the most expansive, creative, surprising and exciting space to live from. Your intention is everything – when you let go of the need to control how and when, the 'what' will fall effortlessly into your life. That letting go is necessary or you'll stall, drag and stumble into the alternative state, always wondering why life feels difficult and stunted, like you're pushing against a force greater than you. (Hint: You are.)

Miracles collapse time

Now, about the small matter of time. We've both seen in our personal coaching practices the desire in our clients to rush through pain and difficult times. The ache for time to speed up and the pain to be over, like ASAP. And we both know that feeling oh too well from our own grabby grabby no surrender moments. But what we also know from our own experiences is that the nature of miracles – that is to say a change in perception, when fear is transformed to love – is that they collapse time.

Say whaaat?

OK, let us explain… First off it's important to say that if you're going through a sticky spot and there's pain to be felt, it should be felt. There's no use crying ten tears when you need to cry a hundred. That sadness will just stay bottled up inside and leak, or, if you're really unlucky, burst out at inopportune moments at some undetermined point in the future. You don't need to have studied psychology to know that it's healthy to feel your feelings fully, and unhealthy to keep them locked away. On the other hand, you also know that involuntarily opening the salty floodgates in the middle of your next über-important client meeting is perhaps not going to stand you in great stead next time promotions are up for grabs.

But, and we'll give you our bona fide #HigherSelfie guarantee on this one, if you're tapped in to that miraculous connection within you – your direct line to the Big U – and are working it daily, the time it takes to move through the pain shrinks dramatically. Staying open and willing and trusting the process of the Universe, and your own ability to work, create and receive miracles, makes 'time' as the world knows it, irrelevant. When you're truly open – and to be truly open you *have* to have a strong surrender practice locked down, it's the only way to stay consistently in the vortex – pain will be felt more intensely, but it will also be released more quickly. (Remember the open palms?) Your ability to move through difficult situations will be strengthened tenfold and you may even surprise yourself with your seemingly superhuman resilience all perpetuated by what the outside world calls 'giving up' but what we know, in here, is the secret to your miraculous strength ;-)

Everything is beautifully plotted for your highest good and if ever there is a lack, you don't need to take the reins because the Universe is literally running to fill the gap. It may not be in the way you expect. It may be filling the gap with the lesson you need to learn to remind you of your true capabilities, rather than, say, a big pot of gold/a knight in shining armour/a goddess on horseback, which as humans we tend to think will be the answer. But regardless, it is always ready to plug the hole with exactly what you need.

> And however much you try, through the need to control or the untamed desire to self-sabotage, to re-route the Universe's plans, the divine GPS is always finding ways to get you back on track.

Jo: In an instant

One of my clearest experiences of miracles collapsing time is how I heard the calling of my life purpose and changed my career path in an instant.

It happened after a really difficult relationship break-up. Things ended abruptly and unexpectedly with my ex's stuff gone by the time I returned home from a business trip and all contact cut, without so much as a 'See ya, wouldn't wanna be ya!' We'd future-tripped heavily together, so when it ended it felt like my future life had been ripped out from beneath my feet.

On that same business trip I'd also been feeling restless about my career. At the time I was doing social media marketing for some of the top life, business and health coaches in the industry. I got to travel the world, see amazing places, stay in beautiful hotels, do fun work that came naturally to me and was paid well for it. But something didn't feel right: I was surrounded by people who were either already doing their life's work or seriously working towards discovering their dharma. On the other hand I was planning a grand exit strategy from my career, which in traditional business terms is a smart idea. But I was planning my exit because I was already unhappy and unfulfilled. I wasn't planning to leave a legacy of something I loved and was passionate about, rather to take the money and run! I had an appointment with my business coach during that trip and I asked her, 'Is it OK that I'm doing work that isn't my life's purpose?'

Cut to me returning home to find life as I knew it devastated. Another divinely timed phone call from my coach led me to Gabrielle Bernstein's book *Spirit Junkie* and from there to Marianne Williamson's *A Return To Love* and then *A Course In Miracles*. It felt like information I'd been waiting a lifetime to read. Everything started to make sense. I read and listened to audiobooks 24/7 and instantly understood mind-bending spiritual theories. I started to meditate and pray and study *ACIM* and, in the wake of what shall hereto forth be known as *that relationship* and the Universe getting the signal from my question about my career, I had a spiritual revelation in my living room #casual. After a really profound meditation I heard a voice that told me my life purpose: to bring spirituality to the mainstream in the UK. I fell to my knees sobbing, saying thank you over and over again. I've never felt anything more powerful or known anything feel truer than in that moment.

I heard my calling in an instant and my question was answered. I fulfilled my remaining social media commitments and told my clients I was changing my business. Within two months I went from being the Social Media DJ to the Spirit DJ. I announced the change via a YouTube video posted on Facebook, put up a new website and launched into my journey as a coach.

As soon as I was ready to open up and truly surrender to the potential for greater fulfilment, passion and purpose – to the potential for a miracle – the stars aligned to collapse time and make it happen for me. The moment I was ready to accept that there was something else out there greater than me working its magic, one of the biggest miracles of my life dropped in – a miracle that had been waiting for me for years.

> The glorious thing about miracles is that they're held in trust for you. You can never 'miss out' on a miracle. They're always waiting for you, whenever you're ready.

So if you're in your dark night of the soul right now, or are still suffering from a shadowy hangover, take heart. The Universe has not forsaken you. It's ready and waiting, holding the space – and all the miracles – for you to open your palms, hand it over and surrender to the awesome plan it has in store for you.

This or something better

Don't tell God you have a big problem. Tell your problem you have a big God. This will chauffeur you from a place of making it happen to letting it happen. It's when we feel most up against it, vulnerable and at risk that our intentions to surrender are most tested, but this is when your reserves of love and commitment, backed up by solid practice, will serve you well.

When in surrender you have to keep your eyes on your prize and not get distracted by what it looks like everyone else is doing, being, saying and achieving according to social media and your ego's wild fantasies. *ACIM* teaches that we must only take our own inventory, which in its infinite wisdom covers a lot of spiritual ground, but one interpretation is that it means no comparing. Stop taking your friends, and colleagues, inventory, because that's not your job. The Universe has a grand plan for all of us. Yup, even your arch nemesis from school. Even your annoying colleague at work. Even your ex. The sooner you accept it, the sooner you can crack on with being a fully active participant in your own grand plan.

What works for some people is simply not going to work for you – whether that's becoming pregnant, getting a book deal, winning an award, starting a business, travelling the world, losing weight, moving to the city or getting a new haircut.

The timing of our lives is always perfect and what's for us simply will not pass us by – this is a divine universal truth, not a tired cliché.

If you've asked for it then it's been heard and is on its way – the pressure is off and the surrender must be on! It will take as long as it takes. Perhaps it will appear to be much quicker for you than someone else, perhaps it will take years or somewhere in between the two. But however long the Universe decides to work on your dream on your behalf, its timing will be perfect.

As the Corinthians scripture highlights: 'Love is patient. Love is kind.' And yet your ego will test your resolve, your patience will be strained and your ability to feel good for other people's successes in the meantime might full-on evaporate as you're distracted by the world around you and your obsession with how everyone else's dreams are coming true, according to their Instagram feeds.

Your ego will taunt you that you're not good enough and cause you to bitch and gossip that those other people are undeserving, that they've had it easy because their parents are loaded or because they're pretty or because their best mate's cousin's dog is famous. Tut! People and their 'networks'. Don't they just make you sick!

So let's just eyeball that one right now, because we girls (and pretty much everyone else with a social media account) love a projection-heavy feeding frenzy. Pull up a chair…

+ Why exactly shouldn't others have success?

+ Why should you have it quicker than others?

+ Who decided that they have it easier than anyone else?

+ Why would you have been singled out to trip up or fail?

+ What did you do to deserve to skip to the front of the queue?

Get your own

You are absolutely responsible for how this gig called life is going to work out for you no matter what led you to today or the connections of your best mate's cousin's dog.

If you're procrastinating, ignoring your calling or fooling yourself that there is actually a time you'll feel fully ready, then you need to remember there's only one difference between those that have 'made it' and you: they're doing it and you're not.

Only you can own that awkward, cringey truth that has nothing to do with your brand new and small but perfectly formed Instagram following or lack of investment or business cards.

If we're each so unique why should 'it' happen for you the same as it did for someone else? Don't you want your own version of success, happiness, peace and abundance? Then you'd better surrender it over and do what it takes to meet it halfway, in your own way.

One final sentiment from the eternally wise and eloquent Rumi: *'Live as though the odds were stacked in your favour.'*

Because they are.

COMMITMENT ×
DETACHMENT = :)

You know how they (good old 'they'!) say you'll never use algebra again after school? For the most part they're right. Mathematicians, physicists, statisticians and algebra fans everywhere excepted. But we'd like to offer up one of our favourite equations, whether you're a champion number cruncher or not:

Commitment × Detachment = :)

Cute for an equation right?! But still a real brainteaser if you're not familiar or practised in using it.

There is a Buddhist saying that 'all suffering comes from attachment.' As a society we are highly skilled in attachment, ergo, perhaps without even realizing it, very practised in suffering. But what exactly do we mean by attachment?

+ Being hung up on a specific outcome.

+ Getting tunnel vision about something turning out the way you think it should.

+ Getting turned inside out at the thought of getting (or not getting) that job.

+ Sleepless nights over the college place you want or stress-induced meltdowns over finding a new place to live in the precise street where you want to build your new life.

+ Obsessing about how your relationship needs to go, and your concerted efforts to manipulate it.

This kind of mental and emotional attachment is bound to drive us crazy because we're actually throwing all our efforts at, and getting attached to… Nothing.

Excuse us for a moment while we blow your mind, but the past does not exist, nor does the future, except in your head. If you need to prove it to yourself then take it in your hands and look at it.

You can't, because again, it doesn't exist. So those outcomes you had so set your heart and all your available psychical and mental resources on are about as real as Jo's childhood imaginary friend, Jag and the imaginary school he attended, Blueberry Hill.

To release ourselves from this exhausting metaphorical grasping of air, we need to practise detachment. 'Oh so that means I can just stop worrying about, planning for or even thinking about anything in my life and it will just drop right in my lap?' Yeeeaaaah, *sure*.

In case you didn't quite catch the sarcasm in those last italics that is not what we mean. If you stopped reading before said sarcasm, we relinquish all responsibility for you quitting your job/house search/relationship efforts in favour of being a full-time enlightened being. Japes aside, active detachment is a super-important lesson to learn on the spiritual path, and just generally for a happy life, whether you're outwardly 'spiritual' or not.

Focus on the process

The way to practise outward detachment is to switch your focus from the outcome to the process. This is where commitment comes in. Instead of throwing all your energies at a set, predetermined outcome – which has probably been manipulated, twisted or idealized by your ego anyway – you pour your commitment into the process. Instead of being single-mindedly set on *getting* the job, you get excited about sending out amazing applications and turning up with sparkling performances in interviews.

Focus on shining your light as brightly as possible, so that even if you aren't the right candidate for the job – and there is no mistake in the Universe, so if you don't get it, it's not for you anyway – you make such an impression that when the next opportunity comes around, you're the one they remember.

Side note: There is something very holy indeed about making someone's day.

Let go and take action

Actually doing what we're suggesting takes time, trust and a whole lotta faith, especially if you've never done it this way before. The 'world', which is what we'll call everything outside of this book, and other spiritual teachings, tells us to 'take control' and 'make it happen'. Remember back there in 'Surrender' where we talked about 'taking the bull by the horns' and how that, sadly, is the rhetoric of much of the modern Western world? How if you're not taking hold of your life and all that happens in it, wrangling, controlling and manipulating it to the nth degree to get precisely what your ego had dreamed up for you in a crazy future trip – that looks enough like 'success' to your friends, parents, teachers – then you're passively letting life slip by and going nowhere fast.

And yeah, to an extent that sentiment is kind of right. If you think this is your 'get out of being proactive free card', you're wrong. This is not an invitation just to think positive thoughts and 'get in the zone' or something similarly wishy-washy woo woo and all will magically appear on your meditation pillow like a golden egg from God. The difference is in the energy. We're suggesting giving the same amount of commitment, focus, love, good vibes and, yes, inspired action, as you have thrown at outcomes you sought to control in the past, at the process instead.

Got it? Good! But if you're not controlling the outcome, who the hell is? Enter your friend, and some even say omnipresent creator, the Universe! The reason it's so important to get this active detachment lark down, aside from the benefit to our mental health, is because it is just a little bit insane and quite a lot arrogant to think that our tiny human brains could even fathom the possibilities that lie in store for us.

Lucy: The tweet and the queen

One Friday afternoon I was scrolling Twitter whilst squashing a sandwich in my face, as I tried to sneak some semblance of a lunch break into another manic day at my job in an advertising agency. This was a good metaphor for how I was feeling about life at the time – I had started to 'wake up' spiritually but yet wasn't conscious in my life. I zoned out in my scarce downtime to deal with the stress of my work, rushing from deadline to deadline, looking for distraction and a quick fix of self-help where I could find it.

Whilst scrolling I saw a tweet from OWN, Oprah Winfrey's production company, asking international viewers to share feedback on the Life Class series. I loved watching these uplifting episodes online and they'd been like a spiritual drip to my soul, allowing me an insight and virtual connection to like-minded people that I just didn't know in real life at that time.

So I thought 'Why not?' as I clicked on the tweet to the survey. If I could do one thing that day that conveyed my enthusiasm and thanks to Oprah and her team, then that would be a good deed done. No attachment to a result or even expectation of acknowledgement of my entry. She is after all the mother ship of self-help in the mainstream Western world. This is Oprah we're talking about and my reverence for her was, and is, infinite. I filled out the survey and submitted my results with love.

A week later my phone rang with an international number that I thought would be business as usual – I was working on some global luxury brands at the time so it wasn't unheard of for me to take a call from across the pond. But it was far from business as usual. It was a producer from HARPO thanking me for my survey comments and talking through the themes of upcoming shows. Could I relate to those topics? What was my opinion on some of those scenarios? How would I phrase that exactly? Followed by lots of animated talk turning to me and my diary... Was I free on these dates? Could I do a Skype interview (read screen test) with the wider team?

Then it finally dawned on me that clicking on that tweet had led me to be sussed out as a Skype guest for Oprah's *Life Class*, not just to share my opinion. I felt myself start to shake – they couldn't make any promises but they thought I'd be a good fit.

It turns out I was and appeared as a guest in four shows speaking to Oprah and her Goddess expert guest, Iyanla Vanzant – and, ironically enough, about comparison in one of our conversations. Had I not thought 'Why not?' and been completely unattached to getting any kind of result, I know I would have missed this cosmic breadcrumb of an opportunity, not to mention dream-come-true, sonic boom of gratitude to hang out with Queen O. I could so easily have continued scrolling but by stopping and acting with love and detachment, one tweet changed my life and mind-set for good – nobody tells me what's possible or not any more.

Think about it; you, along with your evil sidekick ego have probably done a really great job of holding yourself back or playing small in the past. What on Earth makes you think it would be any different when you're in push and control mode? With all due props to the awesomeness that humans can and do create, we are the taps, not the water.

The Universe has grander plans for us than we could ever imagine. We struggle even to comprehend and accept already inalienable truths, things we have experienced like aircraft flight and things we just know, like the infinity of space. Yet we think we are each the individual keeper of the keys to our own destiny. Like we could come up with something better than the Big U, so you know, we'll take it from here thanks.

> Our mission here is to become the earthly lamp that the divine light flows through. The worthy vessel for all that the Universe has to shine through us. Sounds better than pushing or striving or trying to control our little outcomes doesn't it?

Jo: Making the moves

When we created #HigherSelfie Live, the first ever un-conference we described earlier (*see page 23*) we said all along that whether it was a mega conference in a too-cool-for-school converted warehouse space, with duck gyoza and edamame for lunch (which it was) or 20 people in a hotel meeting room and everyone bringing their own picnic, it was happening. Through those miraculous six months we were determinedly focused on the process, i.e. showing up for it every day and making the moves, as mundane as they sometimes were, but always detached from the details of the outcome. We knew we had been called to do this work so we were prepared to create in the best way we could with the resources we had – which, thanks to our practices of surrender and detachment, were pretty damn good resources in the end!

Start now

One of the most sophisticated forms of self-sabotage is perfectionism. It's such a legit excuse for not throwing your full commitment into the process, but if you're old enough to be reading this book, we'll bet you've got enough life experience to know that most of the time even the stuff that goes amazingly well doesn't always look pretty. That some of your biggest wins will have been gained by walking a winding path, rather than a perfectly straight one. Is that not case in point that you're not meant to wait 'til all the conditions are perfect to make your start but to dive on in with gusto and follow your heart, trusting that any 'detours' along the way are just like extracurricular training camps, tooling you up for all the greatness that is to come?

But why, if the Universe has this grand plan for us, don't things just happen 'perfectly'? Well that's because we have free will. We have this incredibly powerful mind that we may do with what we wish. If we're not tuned in to peace and presence as our default frequency that free will can 'get in with the wrong crowd' (read your ego) and run roughshod over your best intentions.

Jo: The backstory

As I described earlier (*see page 73*). I discovered and acted upon my life purpose in double-quick time and. if you looked at the three-month transformation from social media marketer to spiritual life coach, you might think it looked pretty easy and relatively painless. You might even think a three-month turnaround, however much of a roller coaster, has to be better than 15 years of dull ache in a job you slowly grow to despise, right? But that isn't the whole story.

Before social media was my job. I'd trained for six years to be a designer, lived and worked in London and set up – and closed down – a failed business in textile design. Before that I had my heart set on being a teacher, before that a dancer and long-time dreams of being a model. Somewhere along the way I wanted to be a beautician or make-up artist and in the very early days I wanted to be a soldier! Add to that 20-something years of self-discovery. including swearing to leave university/transfer to a different one and then being totally crushed when I didn't get the grade I felt I'd worked so hard for. and I think it becomes pretty obvious that those three months of overnight easy success took a long and bumpy ride to arrive at!

Our friend and leader in light work, Rebecca Campbell, says 'Divine guidance comes to you as ideas fully formed,' so if you've felt the spark of something inspired, that's your cue to act. Not to procrastinate or work on perfecting your technique or spend the next three years planning when you'll start, but to feel your way into this gift of guidance with a grateful heart and open palms and see what happens. See how plans and ideas develop, while you're working on them – don't keep them for your Pinterest mood board hidden away. Commit to them before you feel ready, share them with people you trust and see what blossoms when you're willing to be a channel for what the Universe has in store for you, today, now.

Remember the inalienable truth:

According to the Universe, you already are perfect because of, not in spite of, your perceived 'imperfections'. How could you not be ready? How could you not be perfect? How could you not be good to go right now? The Universe created you this way.

The best side effect, ever

A beautiful side effect of dwelling in this high-vibing state is that life naturally gets easier as you miraculously become a person that stuff gets done around. When you just do you with love and commitment, free of expectation, people and their light are drawn to you. You'll receive offers of help and expertise, priceless opportunities, connections and collaborations that a thousand years of struggle would have never got you.

But once again, this is a very spiritually active process. To reuse one of our favourite well-worn metaphors – the Universe provides the orchard but you must pick the apples. All that is yours is already here, ready for the picking, in the precise order that would provide for your highest learning – and yes, that sometimes includes pain and rejection, but nothing you can't handle and won't make you stronger. You simply have to be in the energetic space of the person that trusts that the Universe provides and be so lit up by your spiritual and physical actions that those ripe opportunities are clear to you.

Spirit works through other people so an important part of the commitment process is to learn to accept and receive.

As your practice deepens and your light shines brighter, you'll find you become more and more magnetic – perhaps people will add you on Facebook, offer amazing unsolicited compliments, recommend you to their friends, and goodwill and resources will start to come to you from those you might expect and those you might not. It might even feel a bit weird and off kilter when you begin receiving unprecedented levels of support for your endeavours and just your life in general. Relax into it. If people want to help you and it feels good, let them. They were sent to you and you to them. We're not meant to do this alone.

Likewise if you're stuck don't be afraid to ask for help and, at all times, remember presence and gratitude when dealing with the generous gifts of time and energy that others give to you. It can be easy to look over the shoulder of the person right in front of you, zoning out while you focus on that one over there, who you're sure is the right person with the right connections, if only you could just cut this off and, and, and…

You never know who or what might be sent to help you or teach you a valuable lesson, so stay tuned in when you 'fortuitously' meet someone interesting or 'coincidentally' end up at a party with a ton a people in the industry you're trying to break into or you 'just so happen' to get an out-of-the-blue e-mail invitation to a lunch that could just change everything if you really show up for it.

Jo: Enjoying the ride

When I changed my career path and out of nowhere became the Spirit DJ, I'd never been known as a coach before. Yes I'd been heavily coached throughout my career, and through my business providing social media solutions had worked with well-established life and business coaches, so I had certainly built up a network in that arena (coincidence, or another perfect training programme by Universe Inc.?) – but as far as everyone was concerned I was not someone who gave advice or coaching. And I'd also never been openly 'spiritual'. Hell, before that time I didn't even know I was 'spiritual'. But I was vibing so damn high, and was so in the flow of trust and belief that this was absolutely the right thing to be doing, that I began my journey as a coach in earnest. Let me recap for you: I wasn't yet known as a 'coach', I had no mailing list, no testimonials to go on, no reputation even as a spiritual person – these followed. What I did have was the kind of energy that was so electric that people wanted to be around it. Oh wait, is that the sound of my own horn being tooted? Why, yes, yes it is. But I refer you back to the Spiritual Smackdown on knowing your own greatness (*see page 29*). It's humble remember? Because in the instance I just described, I was simply the vehicle, the Universe was the driver.

Stop struggling

Still struggling to know where that damned orchard is? Get quiet. Whenever you are struggling, the first place to go is your spiritual practice, that is to say mindfulness, prayer, meditation, journaling, your angels, inside. Go within and be still. Struggling can be misconstrued as taking action, but it's not constructive action. It's ego-fuelled action. It's action that looks a lot like action and can appease those around you, and even yourself on a surface level that at least you are 'trying'.

But all the struggle, all the trying does, is exhaust you and convince you eventually that there's no point, it was all futile anyway and you may as well give up. After all you gave it your best and the Universe didn't reward you, so perhaps great love, fabulous health and a fulfilling career were never meant for you anyway. *Sigh*.

Hear this clarion call from two lightworkers to many: stop the struggle and go inwards. Be still and listen to your heart and your soul. *ACIM* says that 'the ego speaks first and the ego speaks loudest.' We say the Universe is the gentle whisper in your ear, the guiding hand on your shoulder, and when you hush the inner chaos you will see and feel those signs because they are all around you.

> Be brave enough to be still enough in a constantly shifting, over stimulating, digital world. Surrender your struggle and commit to the journey. Untold abundance awaits you when you place your faith in the wisdom and love of the Universe.

SPIRITUAL SMACKDOWN: THE NOBLE ART OF TRYING

We know all about this one because we're British. The saying actually should be 'God – and the British – love a trier.' We love the underdog, especially when they're well under. Our stiff upper lip culture (yes, still!) hasn't adapted itself to being an easy lover of life's naturally confident winners.

Jo: Well, at least I tried

I spent much of my late teens and early twenties in the noble art of trying. Stuck in struggle, chasing my tail, working hard, never really getting the results I wanted and having a good old moan about it along the way ensuring I was the *most* fun in the pub! LOLZ!

However, we're guessing it isn't an exclusively British thing. 'It' being the never-ending cycle of small-time self-sabotage that keeps us in our (un)comfort zone, in varying stages of burned out, giving up, soldiering on and trying again. Ugh. Pass the gin.

But hey, at least you have something to tell your parents when you visit! At least you're 'keeping busy'. At least you don't look lazy/like a hippy/like one of those really annoying self-serving people who are generally a joy to be around because they always fill their own cup first regardless of how weird the rest of the world thinks they are for it. Did someone say cup? Where's that gin?

Really babe, it's time. Give. It. Up. Staying stuck in the noble art of trying – and if you're there then alarm bells will be going off so loud in your head right now that you won't be able to hear yourself think – doesn't serve you or those around you. In fact it's one of ego's sneakiest tricks. Ego in full effect feels like a low-level stream of discontent running through the background of your life. Ego loves you stuck in average, mediocre and meh, when life is definitely not terrible but not really fulfilling or exciting either. When you're in crisis you act, when you're in 'meh' you try.

Jo: I smell a trier!

It really gets my goat when people say they'll 'try' to make time for something, or they'll 'try' to work out more, or they'll 'try' to quit smoking or they'll 'try' looking for a new job. Trying, unless it's done in the spirit of a fun experiment, that you *actually do*, and are seriously thinking of taking up if you like it, is such bullshit.

(Like 'Can I try some of your avocado? I've never had one before' and you eat a bit right there and then.) 'I'll try and make time to meditate.' Uh really? How about just diving headlong into that pool and committing to it no matter what? How about 'I will make time to meditate' or even 'I make time to meditate.' Now there's a statement with some weight, intention and truth behind it.

I can smell a trier a mile off because I used to be one (see above). Here's my hot tip for all you noble triers out there. Give up all the stuff you're 'trying' to do because you think you should and get on with the stuff you actually want to be doing, with love, commitment and passion, no half-hearted trying required.

CONNECTION: PLUGGED INTO LIFE. HARDWIRED TO LIGHT

Having a good connection goes way further than a buffer-free Netflix experience thanks to four bars of WiFi (but obviously we love that too.) You are connected to your highest self because you were born. We're each as connected as each other, like, period. The end.

So we may as well all get over it – we're all connected whether you have letters after your name and an ashram loyalty card or you've just 'woken up', have a meditation app on your iPhone and feel like you might be the only hippy in the village. It's just too outrageous to think that the Universe gives preferential treatment to some over others. We all have the same seeds within us, the only difference being how we choose to nurture and grow them.

True, authentic, solid connection allows us to hardwire ourselves to light, leading to the most productive, fulfilling results in the workplace and workouts, the happiest friendships not to mention electrifying relationships.

When we approach connection as an opportunity really to 'see' each other, with true vision, and show up authentically, with ego on its tea break, we encounter the win-win-win nature of the Universe. But, all this true connection business can be easier said than done...

'I just can't seem to find anyone on my wavelength.'

'He doesn't seem that into me...'

'I think I've grown out of my high-school friends.'

'Where the eff is my effing soul mate?!'

'What does she have that I don't?'

If any of these frustrations sound familiar then you've probably experienced feeling disconnected at some time or another, but whatever your chosen beef with the Universe, the thread all these complaints have in common is that they see us looking 'out there', and putting the onus on others to bring connection to our door. Yet often, we're not willing to get out of our PJs and meet the relationships and opportunities we want halfway or shock horror, offline IRL!

In this modern age it can appear that it's never been easier to be connected – a celebrity might Tweet you as easily as you can get a WhatsApp from your friend on the other side of the world – this connection stuff is easy, right? I mean, surely the theory of 'six degrees of separation' has imploded thanks to the Internet?

Against the backdrop of an ever-shifting modern world, bombarded by the latest news, the latest trend, the latest gossip, connections appear to be happening all the time, and for we digital natives the word 'connection' often goes hand in hand with being online, plugged in, scrolling social media channels, keeping up, observing, swiping, blocking, following, double tapping and on and on.

In all of the noise, chat and puppy gifs the challenge is to be conscious and mindful enough actually to have a genuine exchange – to show up and be present for someone whether they're online or face to face in the pub. How can we sort the genuine and enhancing relationships from the fake and vapid when we have invitations to connect coming from every angle?

Well, it starts with you. Which is the blessing and also the work! We're all here on earth on assignment after all, as is also promoted by our home girls Doreen Virtue and Gabby B.

In the process of waking up to a more intuitively aligned way of life it can take a bit of time and practice to energetically wipe the slate clean, to help create the conditions for what we want to fall in, and for our relationships, no matter how new, to stand a chance of flourishing without our meddling.

'Errr, yeah, OK. I meditate before my Tinder date and I like all my favourite blogger's IG pictures. I think you'll find I'm acing my worldly assignment!'

And yeah, that's all great practice, yet we can guarantee there are places you could use a bit more of an energetic sweep-up to make your connections even more true, genuine and mutually awesome. We need to address the grabby, ego vibes that are whirling around the globe right now, prompted by the rising up of the collective ego and helped along by our shared social media obsession. And the spiritual scene is *not* immune.

It's to be expected that our lives as corporate players, business ladder-climbers and status-meeting attendees spill into our spiritual ones sometimes – namely in the language and exchange of favours for results.

We're not bashing the fact that many in this burgeoning spiritual scene, including us, have come from a background of 'normal' J.O.B.s and suburbia. In fact it's the powers to communicate, organize and plan, learned in conventional workplaces combined with the more ethereal powers learned on a meditation pillow that mean that this movement is mobilizing and the perceived outposts (that is every one of us) are linking up, meaningfully.

The thing to be aware of is the lower-vibe, egocentric habits of pushing, managing, controlling others and sticking to old-school paradigms of getting shit done that can lead us to leak funky energy into the parts of our lives that we need to keep open, clean and 'grab'-free i.e. our spiritual experience as a soul dressed as a human being on Earth.

Too often there seems to be a false need, desperation even, to make, use and manipulate personal connections in the spiritual world in order to benefit, stand out and get ahead – whether we're taking money for our light work or not.

Lucy: Getting in someone's face won't get you anywhere

A big part of what we do at #HigherSelfie is delivering modern, spiritually themed live events. For each one we spend a lot of time scoping out the topic and designing the content. We handpick and pitch to collaborators and at our own expense visit venue after venue to make sure it's just right for the #HigherSelfie high vibe that people have come to expect from us.

Once we've done all that work behind the scenes including late nights, long Skype meetings, negotiating and *all* the spreadsheets, without fail, when we first share the details of the event on e-mail to our online community we'll get a handful of replies back, almost immediately, with really grabby, assumptive, hard-sell paragraphs from those that want 'in' on what we've created. For them, *we're* perceived as the ones to connect to and key to them getting in front of a crowd to climb their chosen pole, via our event. Just minus the work, time and investment it takes, because hey, we've done the heavy lifting for them! And let me tell you, reading those e-mails feels gross and comes with a sharp intake of breath (and sometimes a LOL!) from us. It's polar opposite energy to a genuine offer of help or added value made with love and the intent of true connection – thankfully we get a lot of those e-mails too!

It's impossible to have an authentic connection when the smell of someone's ruthless ambition makes you dry retch. It's a bit like we're applying the rules of the sometimes cringeworthy networking events from the corporate world in the wellbeing sphere.

We've been at 'spiritual' events where people have been getting the sweats to force on us what they do, what they're into, their mission, subscriber numbers, book deal conversations, you name it, and we only asked them where the loo was! That wasn't a conversation, it was an unsolicited consultation with a dollop of weird vibes, dude!

Sometimes the spiritual scene on- and offline seems to be a hotbed of pushiness, which is beyond ironic. Aren't we supposed to be the sage burning, yoga posing, chilled-out ones? We're being called to be the change we want to see in the world.

We can't help feeling that the gross vibes and pushiness come about because there's a false belief that as the 'new age' scene burgeons there's a perception that making the 'right' connections is vital so that there's a slipstream to fly in. This has seen a Tinder-dating mentality creep in, counting people in and out based on their social media numbers or image alone – like they lack credentials or interest at first glance because they're not into taking selfies at every meeting. (*Ahem, guilty!*) We need to move away from sizing each other up to a place of mutual support, like, NOW.

If connection is there and meant to be you can't force it – thank goodness. We're not at school any more and you do *not* have to go to that girl's house for fish fingers and chips to be in the 'cool gang'!

We're not entitled to anyone's time or attention just because we're super-passionate about our thing, we have a million IG followers or once had dinner with that 'guru' back in the day.

This is not, after all, the corporate world of exchanges, gentlemen's agreements and nods and winks where we have to scratch each other's backs and be in a constant state of exchange and return.

Everyone deserves to be acknowledged and appreciated, but you may not get it in the way you demand or pre-design it – the same rules apply for Deepak Chopra and Lady Gaga so you're not being overlooked and the odds are not rigged against you.

So how do we create the conditions for authentic connection, acknowledgement and recognition? All you can do is show up and serve without expectation, otherwise you'll slide down the greasy pole of your own making that you just worked so hard to climb up.

When we were planning #HigherSelfie the world's only spirituality un-conference, we knew it would be right if ten people turned up or ten times that. In honesty we didn't care – our egos were not invited to that party – we just knew we had to try and do something different and game changing. We were in service to the idea and divinely guided just to experience whatever we created without entitlement or expectation. We showed up.

Result? Capacity sell-out with little marketing, our first book deal, and the creation of a spiritual lifestyle company… No pole greasing required ;-)

But what if you feel you don't have anywhere to show up and mingle and serve? In that case you need to create it proactively – like ASAP. By the end of this read we intend to have 'Don't wait for it. Create it.' ringing in the ears of lightworkers across the world!

A rising tide lifts all boats

We're so much stronger when we're acting as one together and #HigherSelfie the un-conference called for us to put on the experience that we'd been searching and yearning for.

Sometimes to create and hone those on-vibe connections you have to break from the pack.

Now, that doesn't have to mean putting on a huge event, but it does start with listening to your soul's calling, acknowledging your area of interest and taking a step to bring that into the world through spiritually active intention.

You need to start talking about what you think and feel about the world, and sharing your perspective wearing your invisible lightworker cape if necessary. A tiny increase in your own light's visibility will feel like a glowing beacon for others – the time for hiding is over and it can no longer be reliant on your made-up measure of success.

> **By just starting to create your own corner you make a space for others to connect with your light – and their own – too.**

You might not impress anyone, you may not get a front cover, you may not be invited to go on TV or to hang out with Oprah at one of her beautiful sweeping estates… Or, you just might! But if your motivation is attached to these ego jewels from the off then it's time to take a breath, because you're setting yourself up for that fall that is so guaranteed after pride.

To paraphrase our BFF *ACIM* let's get a *reeeewind* to the universal truth that 'None of us is special and each of us is special.' So you're as worthy as the next person – no more and no less – and your journey to greatness will, and needs to be, your own.

> **There's nothing more powerful than feeling part of something – you don't have to be the leader just because you were the initiator – the pressure is off!**

> **Your people will find you when they're ready but you have to be there to be found, which is why getting started on your own thing is so important.**

That could mean creating a Facebook group where you and the other high-vibe people in your life share affirmations and full-moon rituals or creating a Meetup.com group for a monthly IRL hangout in your local café or even just your living room.

We wouldn't bang on about this so much if it weren't for the fact that it's exactly what it took to get us to where we are today – no slow burn, no long tiring struggle, no power plays, no overthinking, and definitely no schmoozing or crawling into places where the sun don't shine!

Not everyone will want to join you. It's impossible for everyone to love you – you are not Nutella! To resonate with some and not others is OK – in fact it's great! The more clearly and confidently you stand in your message – whatever that is – the easier it is for the folks who want and need to be in your squad to find you. Likewise it's great for those who aren't a match, so they can look elsewhere. You mustn't dilute your approach or message. A confused mind always says no and we need you, and your tribe, to be a 'YES!'

Connection in your personal circle

A serious and growing problem that seems to crop up, especially in our twenties, is the shifting sands of friendships – connections that were once rock solid, consistent and nourishing simply stop being so, and instead are replaced by frustration, blame, expectation and drift. We can feel really threatened when our social circles change without our consent.

The thing is, as painful as this truth might be, not everyone is supposed to hang around forever and be a permanent part of your circle – can you imagine how exhausting it would be to give real value to all of the people you've met and felt connection with at one time or another throughout your whole lifetime?

We're forced to self-select sometimes and at other times the choice is made for us and there's nothing we can do about it. Iyanla Vanzant once spoke about this to Oprah and she put it much better that we ever could: 'People come into your life for a reason, a season or a lifetime.'

Drop the mic, right?!

People always leave us with a lesson and that insight is a precious gift, even if it was delivered via an angry text message exchange. When apparently loyal, long-standing relationships fade or disappear it's easy to feel it as a loss and take it personally, and yet, the space left is almost always making room for something more fitting, nourishing and authentic for you and your life right now. At the end of the day, if the status quo isn't working for all parties then it isn't working and it's time to give thanks for what *was*, whilst acknowledging what *is*.

Sometimes we're 'ghosted' by friends or lovers – when the person just kind of disappears and shuts down on us – and it's confusing and hurtful. So how do you forgive a friend that ghosts away from your life? The life coach Ryan Weiss has some perfect advice for this and I'm afraid it doesn't include anything as bitchily satisfying as blanking them in public!

You have to send love. It calls for only love and a commitment to seeing their innocence as a fellow soul. This doesn't mean you have to be cool with their actions but you have to accept their innocence and stay high and elevated. Bless them and be on your way.

The world just cannot afford for you to be held hostage by a grudge – in case you missed it before, we *need* your light.

When you're the 'weird woo-woo' one

If you're like us, there's a good chance that you're the buddy who comes with a friendly but seemingly necessary preface before being introduced to a wider circle.

'I'm bringing my friend Lucy, the one who speaks to angels and always asks what star sign people are… But she's an amazing cook and loves to party so she's cool!'

'Yeah I invited Jo… The one who calls herself a spiritual DJ and is always banging on about miracles… But she's great fun and has hipster hair so she's cool!'

When you 'wake up' to a more mindful spiritual approach to life there's a good chance that it will ruffle the feathers of those who knew you before you were 'woo', so prepare for some shift work. You're about to break out of the box and not everyone is going to get it or like it.

Yet, despite this risk, if you want to make the move from fear to love then it's never been more important to start bringing your spiritual, high-vibe habits to your everyday life. In other words, if you're not taking an active part in moving the whole human race closer to love, #casual, by being your most spiritually aligned self, despite what the haters might say, then you'll be disconnected from your true self and wearing that mask is going to feel suffocating and heavy, fast.

We must start bringing all of ourselves to the party – literally in some cases.

That doesn't mean holding unsolicited aura readings at your manager's birthday drinks but it does mean bringing love to every situation and not leaving your angels or spirit guides where you locked up your bike or parked your car – they have to come too. If you leave them behind you'll affect your overall wellbeing – that mind, body, soul connection needs your conscious care.

Abraham Hicks' teachings tell us that our wellbeing is the beginning of all things as it's how we become a vibrational match for our desires. You're the only one that can put yourself on either a wonky vibration or a harmonious one. This in turn will determine whether you feel connected or not. So check in with a vibrational audit by asking the following questions.

✦ What's your dominant vibration?

✦ What's most active within you?

+ Think about your connections – what words would you use to describe them?

+ How relaxed and content are they versus anxious and expectant?

+ How does that make you feel?

+ What can you do to keep your vibration consistently high and in tune with the connections your soul seeks, even when the opportunity isn't obvious?

For example, it might be you work as a receptionist or an accountant. A role that, on the surface, seems resolutely 'unspiritual'. I mean, where's the potential to wear your galaxy print yoga leggings or play your angel-inspired Spotify playlist in a science lab?! Yet there are heaps of uniform- and music-neutral options that will allow you to work your light and create deeply meaningful connections. Sure it might take a little creativity, but that's the fun part!

Lucy: Staying plugged into the light

When I was working in advertising, at times the pressure was intense, which naturally had an effect on how people interacted with each other – I personally spent a lot of time crying in the lavatory. As I started to become more spiritually active in the workplace, there were a few raised eyebrows but people got used to it – my commitment to keeping my vibration high and being plugged into my light had a positive effect on them too. It's all energy, after all. I knew I was starting to create the change I wanted to see when even senior people in the agency would talk about 'sending good vibes' to difficult clients in order to encourage a good result, and one workmate even borrowed my rose quartz crystal to take to her pay negotiation meeting! These little expressions of myself really helped me feel connected to my work and the people around me – the political bullshit and stresses that were once par for the course melted away.

Romantic connections

We are each responsible for the energy we bring to any situation and expecting other people to bring us what we're looking for, including an introduction to our potential new squeeze, is getting us nowhere fast and keeping us single and not so ready to mingle.

Since when was *your* life someone else's job to do?! It's hard enough to order your sandwich exactly as you want it these days so why should you be able to vacuum pack the characteristics of a future lover?

Much of the interference that gets in the way of us connecting with a potential love interest is self-generated. Bummer! Or maybe not... Because you created it you can totally flick the switch on your intention and leave needy, expectant and desperate at the door. It starts with opening up and a good chunk of surrender to clear a path for delicious deep love to show its beautiful glowing face.

Your twin flame might be walking around in Nike high tops but you're looking for a New Balance kinda hipster kid. Is footwear really that important when you're bare-toed in bed after an all night under the sheets bliss session? Nope, thought not!

We need to lead with love and be willing to let connection unfold naturally, without a timescale, a list of expectations or pros and cons. This is when the breadcrumbs that lead our souls to meet will appear.

HANDLE YOUR SCANDAL. SAVE THE DRAMA FOR YOUR MAMA!

Who's the drama queen in your life right now? Your mum? Brother? Boss? BFF? Spoiler alert – if you're struggling to think of someone it could be you!

Have you ever experienced a sense of this? Where you always seem to be party to, or at the centre of, drama? Like there's a repeated pattern of seemingly random bad vibes crashing into your life? For example you have a volatile friendship with your BFF, you switch jobs regularly, you text exes when you're drunk, don't plan your diary properly and mess people about or you slip up at work and bad-mouth a colleague to cover your own back? It's stressful and exhausting to be caught up in, not only for you, but for your long-suffering loved ones whose ears bear the brunt of the latest tale of drama.

Drama, whether we feel we've been sucked into someone else's or knowingly stirred up shit for ourselves, almost always ends in tears and can threaten our chances of happiness, yet too often we look on and just let it happen – that's life, right? Wrong.

One of the promises of this book is to help you 'Wake up your life' and to deliver on this we simply have to cover the grizzly subject of self-created conflict so, drama queens everywhere, get down from your throne as we're here to collect your crown (which by the way is sooo not a good look).

Drama doesn't follow anyone around and it doesn't have favourites.

It's not them – it's you. It's not your hormones – it's you. It's not mercury in retrograde – it's you. It's not 'just my luck' – it's you. It's not the tone of their voice – it's you. It's not his attitude – it's you.

A brutal point to drive home is that we are responsible for ourselves and, with that, how we show up, receive and respond to all the situations in our lives.

Nobody forced you into drama

We, as the human race but especially as a growing army of grass-roots lightworkers, have simply got to get a grip on this self-sabotaging behaviour, which we accept way too easily and somewhat dangerously, as normal. It's the easy-to-hide low-frequency bitching, gossiping and stirring that takes us outside of ourselves and our ability to choose led by our highest intentions: our #HigherSelfie

Drama, scandal, conflict and self-created shit storms can show up in a melee of ego-driven action, under all kinds of guises. The squirm-inducing roll call includes, but is not limited to...

+ Cheating on a partner.

+ Trying to steal someone else's boyfriend.

+ Accusing someone of taking what was yours.

+ Posting passive-aggressive updates on social media.

+ Passing comment on something that is none of your business.

+ General interference in other people's lives.

+ Texting him/her too much.

+ Playing 'hard to get'.

+ Snooping through people's phones.

+ Trolling someone – either someone you know or a celebrity for LOLZ – on social media.

+ Stirring shit up in a sensitive situation.

+ Saying sorry or accepting an apology but not meaning it.

+ Telling lies – little white ones or whopping big fibs.

+ Blaming or scapegoating others.

+ Sharing unsolicited feedback on someone's outfit, personality or worse, their driving!

+ Sending an angry, shitty e-mail when a short, plain-speaking phone call would have done the trick.

+ Indulging in low-vibe behaviour while being well aware of the negative consequences.

You may have been on the giving or receiving end of these scenarios and could probably add a heap of your own anecdotes to this list of cringey upsets. When we willingly participate in these sorts of activities we are totally in an ego headlock.

Any. Single. Thing. That is low-vibe and ego-fuelled has the potential to spark drama, especially if it meets with the touch paper of someone else's ego.

What you may notice about this list is that the scenarios all need other participants. We simply have to have other people involved to get a really good drama going. By them mirroring back to us those aggro vibes we can really suffer and lead from a place of fear. Game, set and match ego!

Think about it – sending a bitchy text to yourself won't have the same effect as firing it at your now ex-BFF. Similarly, publicly blaming someone via Facebook is all the more juicy when the faceless spectators of your social media feed start commenting – drama loves company! We sometimes can't help but drop our little drama bombs because being right and having attention whatever the consequences is like, totally worth it, right?

It's not fair!

When things aren't going right in our relationships with ourselves and others and we find ourselves at the sharp end of people's actions and opinions, it can be really easy to feel like we're the victims, that the world is against us or we're being 'picked on' unfairly. But that victim mentality, created by ego to keep you safe, is all part of its sneaky game.

Blanket statements like 'Why is she *always* such a bitch to me?', 'Why do I *never* get a text back?' and 'My boss just *does not* give me a break!' start to take root as our beliefs about ourselves, and this is where serious damage can begin as we assume the role of the victim, step out of our power and unplug from our soul's ability to carry us home with every breath.

And once you're on the merry-go-round of victimhood – only one tiny piece of your soul per ride! – it only gets worse. Once you've established a victim mind-set your ego will keep you there by helping you find evidence that it really is you against the world and life's just not fair!

None of us is special or seeks out being attacked – the Universal love that you are connected to is *always* trying to call you back home rather than lash out. But when you're feeling under attack your ego, dressed up as your rational mind, is going to want to 'handle it' and get messy by throwing around blame.

This sees you – the real you – taking zero responsibility for the consequences of your actions. It also ignores the fact you have the power to make the right choice for yourself and others within every single moment.

Lucy: When in doubt, *don't*

I've lost count of how many times I've been on a call to a sobbing girlfriend who, through heaving breaths, is exclaiming, 'Why me… Again?' And almost always it's the result of an e-mail or text they've sent or a remark made whilst drunk, angry or feeling in need of attention. To be totally transparent I've also been on the other side of that scenario.

Once you take action, in any given moment, to stir up drama you'll often get what you signed up for, so why the surprise? Why would blame or responsibility lie with anyone but the person staring back at us in the mirror through eyes running with mascara? You could get caught checking your lover's phone, go behind someone's back, make a bitchy comment, ask people to justify how they spend their time because they should be with you – or you could *not* do any of those things. It's all a choice and the outcome you get will depend on the one you choose. The next time you impulsively rush to attack someone, and invariably through that act, yourself too, take a breath – no drama is always an option too.

You'll always find that we use plain language but it's important to state that we are not oversimplifying here. We know that shit happens in life and it throws up scenarios that are upsetting, frustrating and inspire a strong response. Perhaps your boss really is an asshole, your BFF is a narcissist and your mum actually does have an attitude problem but they, and they alone, have to own their stuff as you do yours.

It doesn't have to be fight-or-flight as much as that primal instinct might pull at you. As intense as a situation may get our earthly assignment is to call in the divine help available to us and to be authentic and honest in order to get to the solution for our #HigherSelfie. The last thing we need to be doing is making a difficult situation worse by taking it to social media, for example. But hey, nobody's perfect, and in the heat of the moment we've all been there...

Escalating it will eff you up!

We're not fans of diluting who you are to fit in or be accepted but the fact of the matter is, we have to coexist on this spinning planet, which means we're required to do our bit and not make things more traumatic than they need to be.

To truly handle your scandal you need to recognize that two reactions are critical when something crappy happens. Your personal response to the act – or thing that is kicking off – and the potential follow-up. We are often standing at the fork in the road when we experience drama – one lane is 'make it better' and the other is 'make it worse'.

Choosing drama and escalating a situation will *always* make it worse and increasingly in this digital age, make your private life a public spectacle.

We need to talk about social media

Your dirty laundry needs to go in the washing machine, not on Facebook. Rants, cryptic quotes, passive aggression, nameless threats and calling out people's behaviour on social media only serve to make you look unhinged.

You gain absolutely nothing from taking your drama to Facebook and recklessly parading your emotions will only exaggerate the already challenging scenario you feel stuck in.

The handful of comments from concerned people in your network might feed your hunger to be seen and heard by others but know this – they will never fill you up, they will never change what happened, and they will never help you solve the problem.

Parading yourself on social media doesn't honour your power, it doesn't make you right and once it is seen it cannot be unseen – welcome to your 'digital footprint'.

We have posted and seen others post things we know would never be said in a face-to-face situation so why do we think it is OK to tap it into our smartphones?

The uncomfortable result, and many of you will have experience of this, is our 'friends' are tuning out, FB culling, unfollowing and clicking 'hide from feed' when they see those types of posts. With this, the pool of people paying attention to those that are using FB to let off steam is getting smaller.

Looking at this as a whole – more of us using social media for an emotional crutch, acting differently than we do in person, acting on impulse and our peers turning away – makes us really worried. The impression we get is the trend is growing and we're losing a sense of ourselves, not looking within to make changes that will help us help ourselves in moments of need, and it has to stop.

We are each too precious, unique and divinely connected to make our life experiences the stuff of gossip and fodder for other people on social media.

Who do you want to be? How do you want to be remembered?

By choosing drama and acting out we are cultivating a generational reputation of being reckless loose cannons, unpredictable and bitchy – not exactly qualities conducive to happy, equitable, stable relationships and the personal growth we are on assignment to complete during our time on earth.

Do you want to be right at all costs? For your social media connections to know you've been let down by someone again and you are so over it yadda yadda blah blah?

Or do you want to like yourself and have healthy relationships with the people that love and adore you, and forget the rest?

You can't tick both boxes and it's time for us to rise up and make a choice to work on our shit *as well* as talk about it with selected buddies – either on- or offline – that can be trusted to see our truth with us, and not drag us down into the muck and mire of another drama-lama-ding-dong!

Leading with an intention of support, love and resolution is the magic wand for our dramatic woes. As Dr Wayne Dyer put it, 'Don't make others' feelings about you more important than your opinion of yourself. If you've allowed negative thoughts to become the basis of your self-portrait, you're asking the universal mind to do the same.'

You can start to release your ego's need to be right with one of our favourite affirmations from *ACIM*:

'In my defencelessness my safety lies.'

From drama queen to cool as a cucumber

You deserve love. You deserve it all – unbridled, intense, overflowing unconditional love in every single area of your life. You deserve relationships that are equal and easy, the kind where there's trust, fun, drunken nights dancing on tables and hungover mornings watching Netflix under a quilt, supportive when needed, free-flowing and fulfilling the rest of the time.

You are the magnet for it all – it is there ready for you to claim for yourself but if you choose drama you'll never attract it – your magnet can't work. The opposite of drama is peace and we want you to be anxiety-free and ready to go from drama queen to chilled-out chick without any loss of passion, personality or spice.

It all starts with your own sense of inner peace and to achieve it you absolutely need to love yourself first. Clichéd perhaps but you won't find us apologizing for that. It's time for us to come home to ourselves and look within for the answers and peace we've been seeking, so that we can properly heal.

Loving yourself goes further than being a verb – it's an acceptance of who you are. It must be more than bubble baths, chocolate and early nights, shopping splurges or spa days.

Self-love is recognizing the divine in us that is an actual walking, talking manifestation of the most beautiful light, perfect in every way (even on a bad hair day with PMT!). Big U doesn't make mistakes and you are its most perfectly imperfect creation with your temper tantrums and penchant for '80s pop music.

But our self-judgement means we find it hard to accept and love all that we are, with all of our colours and rough edges. Take a moment now and ask yourself this powerful question we heard from one of our teachers, Robert Holden: 'What is it like to be me when I'm not judging myself?'

It stops you in your tracks doesn't it? Go back to this crazy insightful question and we'll walk with you to your answer: *What is it like to be me when I'm not judging myself?*

Take a moment to assume the feeling of being free from self-judgement. Take out a journal or tap into the notes on your smartphone to collect this as a reminder to keep with you.

+ How *free* would you feel?

+ How *powerful* could you be?

+ How *uncomplicated* would your life be?

+ What would you *do, achieve or create*?

Take a breath

When we act out in the moment without thinking, that's not the real us. It's us at our worst. The side we wouldn't want our mum, best friend, mentor or child to see. That impulsive zing of rage, that confusing maelstrom of accusations and pointy fingers is not who you really are.

When you next encounter an opportunity to create or participate in drama, pause and take a breath. Let the intensity of the feeling pass over you – because it will pass and you will handle it. Show up for yourself like you would for your best friend or your favourite workmate. By lashing out and getting down and dirty with the drama you only hurt yourself. Give yourself the gift of calm. You can and will make it through whatever is troubling you. You may have even experienced the sweet relief of letting the drama drop before. Remember that, and know that this time you get to do so with clarity and awareness that you chose again.

See it all the way through

If you lash out, whether actively or passively, that comment, eye roll or social media post won't go away. Even if deleted it will still have been seen and noted by those that know you. Whatever you put out there, judgement has already been passed. Try this on: see it all the way through to after you've clicked 'post' – there are consequences to our actions, including hurt feelings and misunderstandings.

Is that what you want? To be another blade in an already sharp world?

As real-time and seemingly transient as the Internet is, that will be part of your digital footprint. Over time, a picture is built of who you think you are and *you* are the one influencing that. What we must understand is that the words we use have power. We are what we repeatedly say and it's time to look at whether our words are self-exposing or self-caring and how that affects our digital legacy and reality NOW.

What will your partner, kids and grandkids think when they scroll back in time and read what you're about? When you 'see it all the way through' is it really worth it?

This is not about getting people to like you, or making you more acceptable. This is about getting you to like yourself. You are too beautiful and special not to start to turn up the good vibes and that will give you clarity, serve you and your real truth and protect your self-worth.

Your filter is your friend

Your feelings should not be used as other people's fodder. Yet when we over-share or reach for our drama queen crown we become the topic of pub conversations and bitchy gossip from here to the middle of next week. We filter what we share IRL and on social media as a form of self-care and protection – because there are some things that are sacred to each of us, just for us, too sensitive to be the stuff of public knowledge.

The first of these is our mental wellbeing and how we're doing at a soul level in times when we feel wobbly or insecure – which is more often than Disney movies ever taught us! In truly difficult times resist the urge to splurge on social media and do everything you can to make repairs and get back to strong.

For us this starts with regrouping offline and mustering our support networks for help: cups of tea, strategizing, puppy videos, BFF Skype therapy, beer, pizza, cuddling the dog, whatever it takes. We each forget we have little armies of people just waiting to help us and cover our backs until we're OK again.

There's a saying in the world of coaches and healers: 'Your audience is not your therapist.' That's true for you too, whether your 'audience' is the random gaggle of friends and followers you've collected online or your extended friendship group in the pub. There's some stuff you want to be on the other side of before you discuss it outside of your 'circle of trust'.

Life happens all at once and we must protect ourselves – not out of defensiveness but out of dignity and self-preservation. Your feelings are too important and precious to be the stuff of casual gossip.

By filtering what you share online, you control how you feel offline, and that's more important than any likes, shares or comments someone might tap into an app while they're bored on their commute.

Social media has made us all complicit voyeurs, but our lives are not for other's entertainment. You are one in a million and it's time you cared for yourself that way, you amazing creature, you!

Drama detox

Clean communication means you can be heard even when it's an awkward conversation.

There will be days when you have to climb down off your unicorn and face a difficult, awkward or challenging conversation.

Meditation teacher and author davidji once said that when something shitty happens (our words, not his!) it is 'not an UP-set but a set-UP'; that is, an opportunity to choose to act from your highest good and launch you into your magnificence via another life assignment.

When the time next comes to stand in your power and handle your scandal use your fire to illuminate a way forwards not burn a bridge.

For us this boils down to a few golden rules when we find ourselves in a potentially drama-inducing situation:

+ Keep your language clean.

+ Wait before you respond.

+ State the facts. (As opposed to screaming the judgements!)

+ Invite the other party to talk somewhere neutral.

+ Send them love.

+ Lead with the intention to create a result for the highest good.

+ Have in mind the ideal result from the conversation but don't force your agenda.

+ Listen more than you speak.

+ Imagine the other person as if they were a child or a baby animal – they are innocent children of the Big U too – even if they have just sent you a bitchy e-mail or decided you shouldn't date someone! (Remember they weren't born that way, they've been through shit too!)

- If necessary, consult legal advice. (Not even joking. The Big U made lawyers too.)

- Call in Archangel Gabriel to help support a clear communication and archangel Ariel for strength to stay the course with a pure heart.

Angel homies are the perfect guides to elevate all conversations of conflict.

And remember that *ACIM* teaches that there is no such thing as a neutral thought – you are either acting with loving energy or with fear energy – but there is definitely such a thing as a neutral tone of voice and neutral body language. So keep the physical cues calm and steady while you zap the situation with loving thoughts straight from your Spirit.

Spoiler alert! A final good to know... As the writer and feminist heavyweight Gloria Steinem said, 'The truth will set you free but first it will piss you off.' Living drama-free can take a bit of work to start with but it's always worth it.

TIME TO PLUG
THE BITCHY LEAK

Perhaps your best friend really did lose the weight she set out to. Or you think your lover's eyes linger too long on your BFF from time to time. Or you see that girl on your team at work coming back from another chummy lunch with your boss, and promotion time is coming up. Or you see your ex on holiday with his new squeeze on Instagram... In a flash the touch paper is lit and you're fired up with jealousy: a toxic cocktail of possessiveness, attachment, suspicion and adrenalin-pumping bad vibes.

If there's one thing that girls across the generations have excelled at, it's sizing each other up in the judgement Olympics in order to make themselves feel better. Or, if self-sabotage has taken hold, to make themselves feel worse.

From Queen Victoria's ladies-in-waiting talking shit about their love rivals over a century ago, to Internet trolls maliciously critiquing Kim Kardashian's painfully perfect eyebrows, whatever the subject, a jealous mind is the ego in overdrive. It's out to manipulate us, keep us separate and pitted against each other.

A pattern of acting out of jealousy can often start in school where petty teasing of the girl that has a nicer pencil case turns into bullying, and as we get older it evolves and gets more sophisticated, taking the form of talking behind people's backs, acting passive-aggressively and even escalating to manipulation, sabotage and interfering in the lives of others.

Whether it's expressed outwardly in a rant behind the perceived offender's back or is in action silently via eye rolls and leaving texts unanswered, the resulting bitchy behaviour that jealousy leads to can make us sick at a society level. Not to mention the gross personal vibes that emanate like a bad smell from anyone stuck in the cheap drama of Bitchville.

Jealousy serves to separate and is one of ego's trump cards to keep us disconnected from each other and, more crucially, from our higher selves.

Whatever the trigger, it's time to show up to the lesson

As a lightworker and human being you cannot sit this one out. If you want to create a meaningful and soulful existence, you can't pull a sickie on life to play truant with your ego. To free your soul you have to step down from the envy stakes, learn to choose again and replace those little (or, let's get real, not so little) rages.

We can be complex creatures and often we just can't seem to get behind, or truly and wholly celebrate in others' success. But why is it so hard to cheer for another person's win without the jealousy hangover?

There's a widely held false belief that success or 'making it' in life is a zero sum game. That is, a gain or success by one person must be matched by a loss for another person i.e. you.

So many times we find ourselves getting psyched up when it comes to an opportunity; 'This is IT – it's make or break and I better not f*ck it up!!' Swiftly followed by the ever-supportive internal 'Or else!' Or worse, perhaps, when we choose to believe that someone else bagging a success means that we lose out, or that there's somehow less for us, then we're on the high road to nowhere, ignoring the facts in favour of buying into our own disaster daydream that inevitably ends with us dying alone – 100 pet cats optional. And yet, we couldn't be more wrong.

Unless we've missed the memo from the Universe, we *never* have just one chance, even if it sometimes feels like that.

In our ego's rush to get us stuck in the one-time only or envy trap, we ignore what we know deep down – that there will always be another option – or, breathe deeply now – a little wait for the right thing to come along in its own perfect timing.

There will never be just one person for you, your eternal twin flame, who is so unfathomably essential to your happiness, that if it doesn't work out and they marry someone else, *Four-Weddings-and-a-Funeral* style, you're condemned to a life of singledom and celibacy, with the aforementioned 100 cats.

Your chances of career happiness are not solely dependent on *that* interview, even though you've prepared so much you've memorized the entire company's history and you know the inside leg measurement of the guy asking you the questions. (Oh and by the way, the outcome isn't yours to decide anyway. Kind regards, the Universe xo.)

There will never be just one chance to get a client or a piece of media coverage to get your business out there. Just because your first, second or third pitch got passed up, it's not a sign from the Universe to take down your website and go back to your old job. Your self-nasties don't want you to know that though!

Lucy: Riled and ranting is not a good look!

During the creation of #HigherSelfie, before the hit of Big Magic had fully dropped in, the brand strategist in me spent time researching other spiritual brands and peeps in the industry. Oh did I say 'researching'? I meant my ego was keeping tabs on people!

After a particularly intense day staring down the torch of my Mac, I saw someone post some news on Facebook about a business win. They'd been triggering me for a while and I was in full-on self-righteous jealous mode – they couldn't breathe without me clenching my jaw and getting an adrenalin rush of bad vibes. Well, on reading that Facebook post I went, what the dictionary would define as, apoplectic. I pushed my chair back from my desk and ran – yes, actually ran – to my husband's office effing and blinding and pacing around like I was possessed. He looked on in shock as my tantrum continued towards the ten-minute mark!

In that moment I was in the clutches of the 'zero sum' trap with the belief that because they had something I wanted it meant it was not an option for me – gone in a puff of smoke! I think I may have even started a WhatsApp group to take it further – I mean, I lost it back there. The only thing that calmed me down was to take my dog, Roe, to the beach for a brisk walk where I shouted out loud 'Only love is real!' over and over as if to chant myself out of the jealous fix by the powerful vibes of the famous *ACIM* quote. It worked!

I did eventually simmer down, apologized to my husband (checking his Google history in case he'd searched 'divorce lawyers' LOL!), and deleted the WhatsApp message in shame at my outburst.

I very rarely experience jealous pangs these days as I quickly go to 'Only love is real' and my track record is one that I can draw on as evidence that I *will* figure it out and the Universe *has* got my back. But the triple Leo's rage in me took some taming to get me purring again and not doing my best impression of the girl in *The Exorcist*.

Ego is a bitch too

Ego – remember that little shyster?! – loves it when you're stuck in a low-level stream of discontent, and jealousy and bitchery are one of the best vehicles to get you there, pronto! The reason ego loves you stuck here is because when you're on a high, ego is not invited to the party. Boo hiss, sad ego. When you're in full-on-hit-the-floor crisis, you'll do something about it. But when you're just plodding along, feeling a bit 'meh', a bit crappy, a bit confused, you're not changing anything fast.

Personally, we're not believers that the ego is something to be embraced or befriended, rather something to be accepted and aware of. It's a part of our human nature. And if we absolutely had to put a positive spin on all its sneaky trickster ways we'd compare it to an overprotective parent. Essentially the work it does keeps you small, safe and close to home (read comfort zone) but in doing that it also keeps you from flourishing.

Just like a helicopter parent is there to point out every single danger of a summer sabbatical travelling Europe, from realistic concerns to 'have you been watching *Taken* again?' proportions, the ego is there to bring up every single reason why 'It's not your time', 'You're not ready', or 'You're not beautiful/clever/ funny enough to get it anyway.'

Or even 'You're too beautiful/clever/funny for *that*.' Oh yeah. The ego works both ways baby. In fact it will work any damn way it can. That's why it's so important to stay on your game spiritually.

So, as if to prove a point, we lovingly challenge you right now to think back to what's brought you here, where you are in this moment. When things haven't gone your way in the past or you've seen someone else run off with what you thought was 'your prize' via a braggy Facebook post, we'd bet our bottom dollar that it will more often than not have made space for something that suited you better, felt more authentic and bridged you to something *waaaayyy* more exciting and expansive. *Even* if it felt like the world was crashing down around your ears at the time.

Sometimes we're so obsessed with, and attached to, the way we expect and want something to turn up in our lives, (Dear Universe, I know you're the omnipresent creator and all, but I've had a great idea for exactly how my life should be going right now...) that we miss the fact it's showing up in another way, right in front of us, and is ripe for the picking.

> **Too often we stand in a light-filled room, with our hands over our eyes, complaining that it's dark.**

How to beat the bitchy sweats

Forget the outside glare of social media, pitting yourself against other people and getting distracted by what you *think* they're doing.

Your own unique flavour of success that will fit you better than anyone else, is on its way to you right now. As is so often the case it may have already arrived. It's just patiently awaiting your acknowledgement. Hint: You can take your hands off your eyes now!

Until you've peered through your fingers and seen the light, watch your words and check the energy of how and why you're starting or contributing to a conversation. You may or may not buy into the concept of karma, but let us tell you this: nobody in the history of ever invested anything in a water-cooler bitch.

We may tell ourselves we're innocently asking about someone else's life but if you feel in your gut like you're actually mining for gossip or trying to aggravate a situation then chances are, you probably are, and you'd better get ready because the energetic boomerang is coming right back around. #ouch.

ACIM says only what you are not giving can be lacking in any situation. So withholding love, support and celebration from others is only withholding it from yourself.

When ego has got you in the grip of envy, the light in others can seem too much to handle, and yet the light in them is simply a reflection of the light in you. We sincerely hope you've got the message by now that you are spiritual and worthy and a total gift by the very virtue that you were born. Ergo the fact that anyone is achieving awesome stuff in the world is merely proof that you can do it too. Yes, admittedly some people seem to have a material leg-up in this lifetime with their looks, vast inheritance or ability to speak five languages and play all the instruments, but all those things pale in comparison to the power of each and every one of our individual connections to source energy, and the ability to create and receive miracles.

It's important to remember that your current situation is not your final destination and the same applies to the circumstances of the subject of your jealousy. Life is a wild ride and can take an unexpected turn at any moment for you, and for them too. Everyone has highs and lows, yes, shock horror, even though the lows don't always make it onto social media.

> The key to peeling the cold hard grip of jealousy from your mind is acceptance. Accepting that your path is your own, as is theirs, and divine timing will serve you well, as it has them – especially if you keep doing the real work.

When you can get that last paragraph at a soul level, you can start to be truly at peace with where you are in life right now, and where everyone else is too, and all of a sudden jealousy and bitchery show themselves to be what they really are: a big old waste of a good life.

SPIRITUAL SMACKDOWN: TOO MANY BITCHES SPOIL THE BREW

Stirring up crap, gossiping, manipulating and posting passive-aggressive provocations online deserves a big fat 'no!' The kind you'd give to a naughty dog who's chewing the furniture *again*, complete with pointy finger and stern eyebrows.

The deal is this. Everyone knows everything on some level. Yes, even the ones who you think can't pronounce spirituality, let alone practise it. In fact when it comes to tittle-tattling behind *their* backs, you can be certain they'll smell it like a fart in a lift (or any other confined space you wouldn't wish to be trapped in with foreign flatulence!). You see, folks who don't have a 'conscious spiritual practice' i.e. they too are, of course, spiritual beings having a human experience, but they're just not doing the practical stuff to enhance it yet, tend to be even more keenly aware of the shit-stirring energy going on in their vicinity.

That's because their Spidey senses are still fully functioning like everyone else's, they just haven't found a name for it yet. They don't spend hours pontificating, navel gazing, justifying and internalizing. They can just feel in their gut that uneasy feeling you get when someone's been chatting shit behind your back. You know the one, right?

And we reckon it goes without saying that the more spiritually connected folks in your life will just stop calling if you can't drop the gossip. Meditation takes concentration and commitment and being worried about what so-and-so-said-to-so-and-so-and-yeah-but-no-but is not conducive to a focused practice and peace of mind. #sorrynotsorry.

So next time you're tempted to snark, snipe, snarl or scandal monger, imagine how different you might be if you were made to account for your words and actions and have them live-streamed to the public. Would you still do it? Thought not.

It pays to remind yourself that only what you are not giving can be lacking in any situation. So not giving love, kindness, compassion and instead opting to stir the pot will result in a pretty funky-tasting bitchy brew. Yum.

THE FILTER FACTOR: COMPARE AND DESPAIR IN THE DIGITAL AGE

It can be scary work to announce the dark corners of our ego to the world and, a bit like perfectionism, comparison is a sophisticated form of self-sabotage in our ego's playbook. We do it to ourselves and this truth is as infuriating as it can be liberating.

To level with you, this other 'C word' has the potential to be a great source of inspiration. In some cases, by observing and digesting what is happening to those around us, comparison acts like a mirror of the Universe, reflecting back what is possible in this ever-abundant world – whether that's investing in the new power handbag (yes, that's a thing!), dream holiday (where is my passport?) or simply experiencing the basically beautiful stuff of life that is on offer, in abundance, for free (hello the sound of birdsong or a sexy smile from your crush!). Some people observe others and scroll past, quickly pivoting to a positive thought of 'If they have it then why not me?' and off they skip across their proverbial meadow.

And then there are some people who simply don't pay any attention to what others are being, doing, wearing, achieving or eating, and it has no influence at all on how they feel about their past, present and future so 'compare and despair' is an alien concept. (To be honest, we don't meet a lot of these people, and the ones we do meet tend to be our Nans' mates, whose main point of reference for a life lived online is telling you they saw your cousin's new baby pictures on Facewatch or Lookbook! LOL! We heart Nans!)

But then there are the rest of us, who, if we are really honest, have a better-than-necessary knowledge of where we think we stack up in different areas of life compared to our peers, buddies and colleagues. And rather than using it as a magnetic mirror to call in what we desire, comparison is a corrosive energy that feeds on our sense of worth and can infect our relationships, as well as our ability to follow our soul's calling.

Yes, this ego trick really is that powerful, which is exactly why we need to take off our spiritual, rose-quartz-tinted Ray Bans and stare it down. Comparison, we are coming for you!

The origin of comparison

It can feel almost impossible not to compare ourselves to each other because it's something that's been present since the day we became open to suggestion – literally the day we were born. We get compared to the other babies on the hospital ward when we enter the world and from there, unbeknownst to us, as we grow to walk and talk, we're being sized up, tested, measured, weighed (often literally!) and analysed in relation to our age group.

So a comparison mind-set establishes itself from those toddler-tantrum days, laying its traps everywhere. You might, like us be able to recall growing up, comparing yourself to other people's exam results, sports achievements, boob size, body shape and boyfriends and later, as you became a 'grown-up' with comparison markers expanding to job status, car brand, mortgage, living arrangements, sex lives, handbag label, marital status, Instagram followers, juicing habits, Facebook likes, websites and whatever else your ego could muster to add to the list. That sample in itself is already a whole lot to go at and the potential for self-punch-bagging is huge!

Yet voicing vulnerability and our feelings of uncertainty and inferiority brought about by comparison can be met with a blast of 'get over it' – whether that's because they can't relate or because they can relate all too well and your expression of discomfort pushes some buttons for them that they'd rather have left alone, thank you.

For example, our parents or less digitally inclined peers simply have not experienced comparison to the extent that we do as they've never had to process 'Keeping up with The Jones' on steroids as we have now thanks to social media. Which brings us to a clear realization…

If there's one thing we can all gorge on to keep small and stay shrunk, it's comparison.

One of the ego's chief weapons to keep us in the darkness and shackled to our shadow is to get us to compare ourselves consistently on all fronts. In this state it succeeds in keeping us separate from the universal truth that we are all one, connected and united as a collective consciousness and source of light.

In a world that is brimming over at every turn with potential fodder for our ego's 'scavenger dog', being on watch for comparison is a requirement, not a 'nice to have', if we lightworkers are to avoid its harmful and corrosive effects.

But becoming comparison-free is no easy task at first and nobody gets to skip the work. Not only is comparison an ingrained habit we have practised over time but also, for we digital natives living our lives online, there is barely any respite from the opportunity to size ourselves up against other people.

The power couple of technology and social media means it has never been easier to benchmark yourself against the people you may know well, or by association, and keep tabs on them in a way that just a few years ago might have got you an injunction.

Stalker much?!

As a generation we're participating in 'sharing and liking' or what is essentially mass covert tracking of our friends and acquaintances. And if your feed is anything like ours, on a minute-by-minute basis, you'll see a celebrity's lunch, your BFF's baby, your ex's holiday tan and a workmate's promotion scroll past in just one 'hit' of Facebook or Instagram.

It's all up for grabs when it comes to judging others via our own, individual made-up metrics and benchmarks and they're constantly being updated and reviewed on our ego's 'us against them' virtual scorecards.

We each have our own 'go to' list of people and things that, through comparison, we bash ourselves with, and overlook our chance in the present moment to grow, shift and thrive. Do any of these hypothetical thoughts sound familiar when it comes to what we observe in other people's lives?

'Look at the size of that engagement rock!' – *Hmmm that must mean I really am the only single person in my network... Or perhaps on Earth?!*

'How did he get that weight off?' – *Aha! As I suspected I am a lazy who that will never amount to anything!*

'Shit, look at the amazing press coverage her business received!' – *Got it! All of my ideas are crap and I can never compete with the likes of her sparkly self when I'm just lil' old me!*

'How can her house and children be so clean and perfect' – *Jeeez, why did I ever think I could handle raising a human?!*

When you're not feeling connected and your cup isn't filled, your ego will always have a put-down ready for you.

Cue anxiety, insecurity and feelings of neediness and vulnerability that, faster than you can squeak a dramatic '*Noooooooooooo!*', will suck you into a downward spiral of feeling less than – like you're the only person that doesn't have this thing called life figured out and that you'll never be able to make the transformation you truly desire.

This is because comparison – whether stimulated by social media or not – can lead us to believe that to be successful or accepted we have to perform and conform. And that perceived performance can, in an aggressively oversimplified way, boil down to some key social media 'status updates' that are worryingly linked to acquiring stuff and seeking fulfilment outside of ourselves. For many, these comparison boxes include ticking off jobs, cars, marriage, kids, fancy holidays (or pretty standard holidays made to look fancy), mortgage and the odd shopping splurge – but not before gap years and bikini selfies and wild nights out – repeat to fade.

It's important to state clearly that there is zero judgement from us towards any of those events or milestones. After all, who doesn't love going on a trip overseas or bagging those much coveted Chanel espadrilles? And, for the record, we both have quite a few of those boxes ticked between us but not, we hope you've realized by now, for the superficial satisfaction of ticking the boxes.

We want to shine a light on one of the fallouts of comparison, namely, the perception that it is necessary to tick pre-agreed boxes to 'amount to anything' in your life. Society, including our friends, parents, social media feeds, and the brands we buy can make us feel that if we're not racking up that checklist by the time we're thirty then God help us! Order the kitty litter, old lady, 'cause there's only one place you're headed!

But this is what we like to refer to as 'total bullshit'.

What works for some will not work for you. The timing of one person's relationship start or end will have no influence at all on your own. Someone going travelling for a year does not mean you should do the same when you kind of want to buy a house and start nesting. Whatever your life stage, whether you're starting out in your adult years or deep into retirement and reflection, none of these choices make you more boring or interesting. When made authentically, these choices just make you, you!

> **If you're following a crowd without checking in with your internal compass then your life is in danger of becoming someone else's tribute act.**

You know, like those bands that play famous songs in dingy bars, not as well, not as loud and not in the same key as the original? The ones that have names like 'Mouldplay' and 'Noasis'. Yeah. #lifegoals

If you squint your eyes and muffle your ears it may sound like the real thing but you know it's not authentic or the true article. It's a performance – a copy that takes practice, changing, squeezing and diluting your true self.

When you compare yourself to others and follow what they're doing because you never take the time to figure out what will make you happy, this is exactly what you're doing – putting on a tribute act. It's uncomfortable, exhausting and unnecessary.

You are already a unique act by virtue of the fact you were born.

Compare = despair

Comparison massively affects our beliefs about ourselves, which in turn brings our energetic frequency down. This is the equivalent of locking your potential in a box and hiding it under the bed where it's dark, just left to wane and waste.

What further reinforces comparison's low energy frequency and cuts off any creative energy we can muster to change our perception or circumstances, is the widely held belief that success is a zero sum game – a special bonus gift from your ego to keep things really dark.

We can start to label a win or success for someone else as a loss or failure on our part. This in turn can encourage a competitive or combative vibe towards each other and you may find yourself compiling a panel of likely suspects that you can use to gorge on for your comparison fix.

Lucy: Bigger engagement ring, bigger hair, bigger handbag

My comparison low point occurred when I was about 27. It spiralled into a very dark period in my life that took me a couple of years to recover from. I attended a school reunion that I wasn't that keen on going to but decided against my better judgement to give it a shot. I had a great time on the day – laughter, nostalgia and catching up, over flowing Prosecco. I wasn't in a particularly great place at that time – my now husband's business had gone into liquidation and we were facing losing our house, which we subsequently did. So the aftermath of that school reunion was like a Las Vegas of comparison that I gorged on via social media, becoming particularly obsessed with a couple of individuals who became avatars for what I thought was an unattainable level of success and happiness. Bigger engagement ring, bigger hair, bigger handbag, bigger designer wedges. I used to stalk their Facebook feeds to compare myself and collect the evidence that I'd never amount to anything and that I'd been dealt the bad hand in life.

We all have a version of that girl, guy or group who turn up as a recognized archetype and target for our comparison. He or she will have appeared in different guises through your school years, work life and social circles, and as you read this you can probably picture him, her or them right now. Perhaps it's someone who seems to have it easy, who's lucky, well liked, successful, academic, in love, who ended up with your ex, or seems to find healthy eating a breeze – that someone who, ultimately, we feel is not like us and will always be a stranger, rival or silent conspirator against our own success.

The reality couldn't be further from the truth.

Don't drink the Koolaid! Kick that ego to the curb

Comparison disconnects us from our source because the light that we share is available to us always. Comparison takes us out of the present moment and prevents us from looking at all the ways we can be creative and make space for the miracles we truly desire.

We are each deeply and equally connected, worthy and light-filled, with untold potential regardless of the perceived lucky breaks or upsets that we experience in this lifetime. We can come back from anything and choose again. We can shine even brighter than our last 'high point'. This has nothing to do with anyone else and everything to do with our relationship with ourselves and our intention to be authentic.

We must learn to question the ingrained assumptions that our own world view is the status quo and build our immunity to the ego's trick of comparison.

From compare and despair to #comparisonfree

Whoever is the subject of your obsession or comparison curiosity, in turn, will also have their own panel of people that they voyeuristically keep tabs on, dedicate the odd bitchy comment to (even if it's just in their head) or start a loaded conversation around.

And this applies to you too!

Whether you believe it or not, you too are someone else's benchmark. At your current weight, job, relationship status, haircut, and snazzy new shoe purchase – you are the subject of someone else's 'comparisonitis'.

Maybe you already know it or maybe it seems crazy to you, but it's true. We are all in this together – hungry for connection, togetherness and alignment and now more than ever we each need to heal so the next person can take strength from our own example. This is your clarion call to accept responsibility and strive to live comparison-free, even with the lure of social media tempting you to do just the opposite.

Notice what you notice

It's something that so many of us experience and can relate to yet comparison is still treated as a bit of a taboo subject. Unfortunately this only serves to keep us in the comparison trap and means you never get to the insight it holds, that is so unique to you, and the life you really, authentically want.

If you're comparing yourself to other people, ego wants you to stay in that icky discomfort but at the same time your intuitive voice is inviting you to answer honestly for yourself: 'So what?' – that is, 'What's this trying to reveal to me?'

If you feel like your friend seems to live in the first-class lounge of the airport, instead of dwelling on the perceived 'unfairness' of the situation, take a step back and ask yourself 'So what?'… The answer will come through with some killer, impactful insight that you can use to create a miraculous life in the present. Your 'so what?' in this comparison scenario might be 'I'm so tired, I can't remember the last time I had a break and got pampered. That needs to change.' Notice how that specific insight starts with you and has nothing to do with your friend's air miles!

Everyone has to start somewhere

In the mind, body, soul industry there's the potential for idol worship just as there is in the fashion, pop, technology or business sectors – not helped by a focus and reverence for high social media followings that create an impression of influence and superiority. (Oh hi, ego headlock!)

These pedestals we build in our minds and the media separate us from the teachers and their teachings. Comparing ourselves to other people's progress means we flip the 'off' switch on the shared light and potential we have the capability to harness, no matter where we are on our journey.

There is room for all to thrive but to do so you must use your gifts to meet your miracles halfway. Nobody is immune to admiring, celebrating and appreciating the work of others as they too rise up – even one of our spiritual crushes Kyle Gray has 'spirit junkie', the phrase made famous by Gabby Bernstein, tattooed on his feet.

You are cordially invited to enter a state of becoming.
It doesn't happen overnight or by taking a pill and
whatever you have in mind for your miraculous
life, it's time to start! It's time to become it!

Be more...<canine> [insert your spirit animal here!]

We can take a lot of inspiration from nature in our quest to live #comparisonfree. It's following nature's way that we find our own expression of who we are and how that will manifest. You'll never see a dog trying to emulate a cute kitten for more attention or a robin trying to be more like a mighty eagle. Because they get it's OK just to be – they have a sense of self that applies in every moment. Animals are never challenged or manipulated to think they should be anything else but themselves so they live to the full potential of that without question. They're conscious, but not self-conscious.

So what does this mean for us souls cunningly disguised as humans walking the Earth? It means taking our power back and becoming conscious of the choices we make and how this influences the ecology of our lives.

It means allowing yourself to be you.

So stop saying 'yes' to crappy dates, boring parties, late nights, unfair feedback at work, trips you don't want to go on, relationships that don't serve you, eating habits that keep you feeling miserable. Do what it takes to make your tail wag, to bring calm and rest into your life as well as spontaneity and surprise. You deserve it all on your own terms independent of, and undiluted by, what other people are doing.

Allow it all. Be more YOU.

Forgive yourself

The first impulse when you realize the potential opportunities, time and energy that have been wasted on comparison is to feel regret, frustration and shame at having not chosen a more loving, intuitive approach to life and yourself. For not having had a more consciously self-loving mind-set or not having asked for a miracle.

But, one of the beautiful teachings of Marianne Williamson's *Being in Light* is 'Anything that is your genuine experience is your passage of initiation.' In other words nothing you have said, done or thought to this point has been a mistake. It has actually been part of your training – you just passed your audition! Now you are smart to the ego's tricks you can choose again – in every instance of comparison is an opportunity for you to choose love and accept yourself.

The Universe is set up for you to win in your own way. You are forgiven (and for the record, you never did anything wrong).

It's OK to be a hipster

Being authentic and creating your own miraculous life, whatever that means for you, is actually pretty nonconformist and outside the cultural mainstream of this modern age.

It requires a deliberate and conscious display of your choices whether subtle or overt – it's actually a bit hipster to live authentically. But fear not – expensive coffee, vintage bikes, living in Williamsburg or Shoreditch, and waxed moustaches are all entirely optional. It's the attitude and intention that counts!

It means questioning your assumptions as well as the assumptions of others out loud or just in your own meditation.

> You're not meant to be everyone's cup of tea. You're not designed to blend in, dumb down or dress up to emulate what wider society thinks is acceptable. That will only shackle your soul to an exhausting lie.

Clear up the energy

We've referenced the influence of social media a lot because (in case you hadn't noticed) it's a digital world we live in! Its influences on us are varied and complex, to such a point that it might at first appear that we are powerless to this insidious source of comparison content, but with a little practice we can proactively create a positive relationship with all of those apps!

A digital detox is largely impractical in this day and age so consciously managing your social media feeds rather than blocking them altogether is a powerful practice.

Treat your social media feed like a house party. Don't invite people, stories, brands or news into your life that don't contribute to a feeling of wellbeing and positivity.

Unfollow, put on hold and mute the unwelcome guests that trigger your comparisons (you know who we're talking about!) and actively invite in and interact with the people, brands and conversations that make you feel entertained, inspired and lit up.

SPIRITUAL SMACKDOWN: KEEP YOUR EYES ON YOUR PRIZE

Our favourite phrase when it comes to teaching and practising spirituality, in this modern world full of a million opportunities a minute, is self-preservation.

It's kind of old skool but we're reviving it for the sake of all the spiritual side-hustlers out there who are working their butts off between bridge jobs in the name of all that they're passionate about.

It's scarily easy these days, before you even begin a new endeavour, to hop online, check out the 'competition', convince yourself there's not an original bone in your body, or that the market is saturated, or you couldn't do it as well as 'them' anyway, and wave a white flag at your dreams.

It's too easy to research yourself into a stupor, overwhelming yourself with every nook and cranny of detail there is to know about your chosen field. Finding every course you could do to get better at it, hypothetically spending your life savings on getting qualified out the wazoo before you've actually given it a go and dipped your toe in the coconut water, so to speak.

Both these super-fast Internet-fuelled exercises will only serve to create fertile ground for ego to plant his little seeds of doubt, and before you know it that spark of inspiration that woke you up with a jolt at 3 a.m. or that slow-burning desire that's been eating away at your commitment to your day job for the last five years has been safely dismissed because, because, because…

So we'd like to offer an alternative to all this self-sabotaging and ego enabling. It's called self-preservation. It's called keeping your focus on your thing. It's called get off the Internet, stop looking at what everyone else is doing and get on with your passion project unencumbered by information overload. It's called keeping *your* eyes on *your prize*.

Smart research and due diligence is a good thing whenever you're starting a new venture – and watching a ton of YouTube videos to learn a new skill or hobby is totally cool – but you know in your heart the difference between what's actually productive and what's holding you back.

You see, whether all the amazing, creative, talented people out there (and erm that's everyone, because everyone is creative and talented at something) were doing what they love or not, it kind of doesn't matter. For every person that sits home alone three hours deep into research on why they're not good enough to do anything, there is someone who is breaking their balls to do their thing regardless. And those people who have gone before you don't make it less likely that you will succeed, they actually make it easier.

Here's the spiritual theory behind the real-life evidence:

The Universe is infinitely abundant.

So if you want to be a singer and someone else gets a gig or record deal, it doesn't mean there's less chance of you becoming a singer. The Universe doesn't work like this because nothing is ever 'taken away', only added. So if you think of all the opportunities in the Universe to be a singer as a pie, (mmm, pie!) when someone else gets one of those opportunities, that slice of the pie is immediately 'replaced'. When you approach the pie for a slice, there is just as much as there was when the other person got their slice. In fact, the more people that create from a place of love and joy and inspiration the bigger the pie gets! So by the time you go up for your slice from the buffet of life, there's actually more for you to choose from! Pretty cool, huh?!

So instead of feeling downhearted whenever you see someone else making strides doing their version of your passion project, flip it, with self-love! So what, someone else got press in your field? That's great, it means that magazines are open to writing about what you do! So what, someone else did a super-successful workshop on your specialist topic? That's awesome, it means folks are willing to buy tickets to learn about that!

And a word on originality, because it's helpful and kind to yourself to remember there is nothing truly original left to create. Everything has been done before to some extent. Modifications, customizations and adaptations can and will be made. But as for a truly original idea, forget it! Which, of course, is super-cool because it means the pressure is off. It means you don't need to be the first or the original to get started. You can just be you! Your voice, your style, your tone is the modification, the adaptation, the 2.0.

Thank the lord that Jennifer Lawrence didn't say, 'Well there are a lot of young beautiful talented female actors out there. I should probably just get over it and give up. Plus what's the point while Meryl Streep is alive?!'

And thank heavens that Ed Sheeran didn't say, 'There are thousands of tortured teenage guitar-playing singer-songwriters out there, why bother?! What could I possibly add? And the dude who plays Ron Weasley has already got the cute ginger market cornered!'

Start treating yourself and your side-hustle like you'd treat your bestie and her thing… With love, compassion and enthusiasm. Tune out of the obsessive comparing, tracking, snooping and researching and get on with the business of being awesome. (It's a full-time job y'know!)

Whatever your passion is, practise a little self-preservation and demonstrate your commitment to whatever means enough to you that you turned down drinks with the girls or a Netflix-and-popcorn-a-thon by keeping your eyes on your prize. You totally owe it to yourself, you mystical effin' creature you.

LESS ATTITUDE, MORE GRATITUDE

Jo has her Core Desired Feelings (CDFs) as the lock screen on her iPhone. (The original truth bomber Danielle LaPorte describes CDFs in her book, *The Desire Map* – you should definitely check it out!) At the time of writing, Jo's are:

✦ Abundance

✦ Connection

✦ Presence

✦ Peace

Whether they are bang on alignment with you or you'd choose different CDFs to shoot for, the key that will unlock all of those much-coveted feelings is gratitude. As Meister Eckhart said, 'If the only prayer you say in your life is "thank you", that would suffice.'

Gratitude is more than just exclaiming thank you, *merci* or cheers! It's joyfully accepting what is, rather than wishing we had something else, something more, and something better. It's being thankful for what we have right here and right now. That also makes it the fast track to abundance, presence and peace.

When we're in a state of gratitude we're playing in Spirit's backyard with a free bar, a pool and novelty inflatables, and ego is *not* invited.

Comparison and envy stem from believing that we are all separate, as *ACIM* says, like waves thinking we are separate from the ocean. When we are whirling around in the gratitude vortex we are much better placed to experience true connection, with ourselves and with other people, because we're present, accepting, at peace and feeling abundant. Our vision isn't fogged by the confusion and untruth of separation.

So much more connection is available to us when we are practised in the beautiful art of gratitude. Gratitude not only for what we have personally, but also for what others have too. Often we get caught up in thinking that because someone has achieved something that we desire (or if we're having a really bat shit crazy moment, something that we don't even want, but it's some form of 'success' so ego can latch on to it anyways) that it means there is less for us. What it actually means is that there is more for us.

Someone else getting what you want – whether that's a hot lover, a promotion or getting an interview published in a glossy magazine – paves the way and makes it easier for you to get there too. Yes it's nice to be 'the first', but pioneering is hard slog, and not always recognized in its prime, so if you're not 'the first', that's a whole other perspective you can be grateful from.

Take the spiritual world for instance. Did Marianne Williamson's success make Gabrielle Bernstein's career path harder or easier? Did Gabrielle Bernstein's work make this book more or less likely to be published? There have been times in our individual careers when it's felt like it would be so much easier to just play small and say 'Yeah but... I'm not connected enough, I'm not spiritual enough, I'm not New York/LA/London/Sydney enough...' So thank goodness for gratitude, and the way it opens our eyes to the abundance that we already have.

Yeah but...

If anything will snap you out of a severe case of the 'yeah buts' it's getting into gratitude, which for most of us in the Western world, even when ego would have us think we've got nothing to be grateful for, is pretty easy. At last estimates in 2011, over a billion people in the world live on less than $1.25 a day and two billion more live on less than $2 a day.

So however disconnected and down in the dumps you feel, start here: a roof over your head, food in your belly, friends to confide in and money in your account.

Yup, even if it's only a penny. Yup, even if it's overdrawn, (been there, a lot!) because even when you're overdrawn you still have the capacity and circumstances to earn money to put into an account in the first place, which we're guessing is more than the three billion folks who live on $2, or less, a day have.

And yes, sometimes gratitude can feel like a real self-righteous f*cker, because it requires us to rise up out of our pit of despair that ego has so carefully prepared for us, lovingly lined with all the reasons that we can't, why it won't happen for us with empty spaces carved out for all the things we don't have.

Gratitude requires us to rise above and be our #HigherSelfie: the self that can bask in our ability to create abundance in an instant, our capacity to rediscover peace. Yes, *you* included – you with the overdraft, the unmanicured nails and one tin of beans in the kitchen cupboard. How come? Because you are miraculous by your very existence. All you need do is choose gratitude over fear and lack, and abundance, connection, presence and peace can be yours in a heartbeat.

Jo: Less than nothing

Right after the financial crash of 2008/9 (the year I graduated university, yay timing! LOLZ!) I saw a YouTube video that documented a couple of people who decided to go economically 'off the grid'. I don't remember the name of the video, or the name of the people, but I do remember the 'off the grid guy' in the video saying that right now, having zero, flat nothing, financially, is actually quite a lot. When you think about how many of us casually live on credit, dipping into our temporary loan facilities at the end of every month, spending more than we earn and often not consciously saving anything, it's not uncommon to live in a nice apartment, eat at good restaurants, wear smart clothes every day and actually have less than nothing, less than zero in your account, with bills still owing at the end of every month. I thought what a frickin' killer perspective shift to have when we're thinking about gratitude, and getting real about what we *actually have* versus all the things we think we have, and how we value these two sometimes very different things.

Your upper limit, foreboding joy and gratitude

What happens if you *don't* practise gratitude? Aside from unwittingly becoming one of those energy-sapping people that can drain a room of fun before the first drink is poured, it can seriously hold you back. We're going to create a delicious mishmash hybrid of the work of two of our favourite authors to explain how.

If you haven't already read *The Big Leap* by Gay Hendricks, do that. If you have, we highly suggest rereading it. It contains impactful insight you're going to want and need along this journey we call life.

In the meantime we'll give you the potted version of one of the main points of this incredible body of work. Gay says that we have 'an inner thermostat for joy', i.e. the pre-set amount of good feeling we can take before we do something to self-sabotage and bring ourselves down to a more 'comfortable' level – or rather a more familiar level. This level is pre-set by many different factors including past experiences, your upbringing and the culture and society you come from.

An example of this might be that you get a promotion and a pay rise and you're on a total high, your self-worth is through the roof, you feel gratified that all your hard work finally paid off and satisfaction that hey, maybe you are one smart little cookie after all. Then you come home and manage to start the most almighty fight with your partner/parents/housemates and you're right back down again. Not down to rock bottom, but down to average, back in your comfort zone for joy.

Then we have the work of the incredible Brené Brown, who again is a must-read and a spiritual activist if ever there was one. Her work is vital, especially to those of us who are consciously waking up to the cosmic alarm clock and tuning in to our lightworker capabilities, so please seek her out if she's not already on your Kindle list.

When she's talking about vulnerability and shame resilience she tells of 'foreboding joy'. That is, when you feel a rush of love and joy, because of your conditioning, because of your pre-set upper limit, instead of being able to sit with that feeling, bask in it and enjoy it, you start to imagine all the violent, terrible things that could happen to bring you crashing back down.

Brené Brown says we do this because we're trying to beat fear to the punch. In our most joyous moments we're trying to prepare ourselves mentally for when it all goes wrong – what she describes as 'foreboding joy'. We've been so conditioned to believe that it couldn't possibly be *this good* that instead of being present in the truth that it is in fact, *actually this good*, we borrow drama from the future because we can't stand the thought that we'd be the gullible fool who believed their own hype.

So you can see how 'foreboding joy' becomes the emotional self-sabotage we use to regulate our thermostat for happiness. Brené Brown is a prolific sociological researcher and she says that every single person she came across who was able to recognize and stop 'foreboding joy' had an active gratitude practice. Not just a sporadic Band-Aid style use of being grateful but a consistent attitude of gratitude.

So start now. Don't wait for that awful dark feeling of 'What if...' to creep up and blindside you in your next moment of unbridled joy. Begin building your anti-self-sabotage force field right away. Begin a gratitude journal, take a deep breath and simply say thank you for the day ahead every morning when you wake up. Share the highlights of your day with your friends or family every night when you get home from work, start a gratitude WhatsApp group, say grace before dinner, but for Spirit's sake, just do something.

How to be grateful

Like all spiritual practices (the clue's in the name), gratitude works best when done often and consistently – a bit like those tight buns you're working on at Pilates! Or at least as consistently as you can muster if it's new to you. A concept we'd like to introduce is being a 'spiritual opportunist': start getting really conscious of your spiritual practice so that it's the first thing that comes to mind whenever you have a spare moment or two – yes, above checking e-mails and Facebook – and act on it. It would take you a grand total of about 60 seconds, or maybe even less, to think of three things you're really grateful for, and say thank you to the Big U. Imagine if you started a habit of grouting your day with little smidgens of love and gratitude, instead of micro doses of distraction, comparison and lack.

Try it when you're on the train to work, when the commercials come on between your favourite shows, when you're waiting for a friend in a bar, washing the shampoo out of your hair or on the loo. Because, yes, we know you take your phone to the loo, and we're thinking if you're not concentrating on doing your business you may as well be doing something spiritually fulfilling. Hey, hectic lives, no judgement! LOL!

Lucy: Gratitude – The hot knife of peace through the butter of stress

When we lost our house due to the cumulative effects of, and a spiral of circumstances, directly and indirectly related to, the financial recession in 2008, I had a bit of a breakdown. But by following cosmic breadcrumbs I was led to read *The Secret* by Rhonda Byrne and I discovered the concept of gratitude and the power of 'thank you'. I was able to arrest the stress, hurt, overwhelm, confusion and anxiety in what felt like a heartbeat.

Introducing a gratitude practice to my day created so much space that I no longer felt like the walls were falling in around me. It all started standing in the shower rinsing my hair – that 60 seconds each day stopped my ego sticking its claws in and grappling control of my days as it had got so adept at.

Gratitude does not need to be profound to be effective. Yes it would be wonderful if you could think of really deep meaningful things to be grateful for every time, but sometimes you genuinely are just really grateful for your new Nike Fly Knits, or for a gorgeous song you rediscovered on Spotify or for the inch of ice cream you just found lurking in the back of the freezer that is totally going to make your night (epic win!). Don't judge, just practise and build your ability to find the opportunity for gratitude at every turn.

You are not a robot

Warning: Beware the tyranny of positivity. This call for more gratitude is not a cue for fake smiles that hide tears, and spiritual smugness when a sigh of relief would be closer to how you're really feeling. Being grateful and finding ways to do it more and better does not mean that difficult, painful things don't happen any more, or that you need to be some kind of freakish happiness robot that doesn't ever experience the crappy stuff or empathize with others.

What it does do is make you more resilient and resourceful in tough times. It gives you greater stores of joy and perspective that you can draw on when you need to. It gives you real faith in the ever-Tweetable wisdom of one of our life and business heroines, Marie Forleo, who says, 'Everything is figure-out-able.'

Likewise your gratitude doesn't always have to be metaphorical lollipops and rainbows. We've covered the superficial stuff but sometimes the mundane and mediocre make it onto your gratitude list and that's OK too.

Jo: Gratitude boot camp

Not long after I began my journey into professional spirituality I got put on a crash course of minimum-wage, maximum-hours bridge jobs. I'd had generous enough parents that I'd never had to go there before and I now see that it was a super-valuable lesson for me in humility, productivity and getting real about what I really wanted in life. When you've cleaned the gents toilets in a busy pub at I a.m. for minimum wage, working on your side-hustle website at 6 a.m. before work and then again until midnight truly ceases to be a hardship!

I remember calling Lucy on my drive home from one of my jobs and, although I was exhausted from the effort and unhappy in the work, telling her that I was grateful for the lessons I was learning, grateful for the income it gave me because it helped me to do what I really loved, and grateful for the fact that I was doing what I was doing at that point in my life. I truly felt that I was demonstrating to myself and the Universe that I really meant business because I was totally willing to be in this less-than-ideal situation, if that's what it took to get to here, where I really wanted to be.

So sometimes gratitude isn't pretty. Sometimes, just like life, it can be a bit gnarly and gritty. Sometimes it's about getting present with your ability just to be present, and hold the stare of something that feels uncomfortable, safe in the knowledge that your gratitude will help transform your situation into something better.

No judgement

Being grateful that it didn't rain on your walk to yoga is utterly acceptable and being grateful that no one Skyped you tonight because you were too tired for small talk is good too. In a perfect reflection of real life, your spiritual practice won't always be earth-shatteringly exhilarating but as long as you're spiritually active and willing to show up it will always be worth it, it will always work, and its effects will grow and grow the more you do it. And that's something to be grateful for ;-)

Your gratitude practice will not get you any more Spirit Points for being particularly poetic, earnest or sage. Being grateful that your hellishly long workday is over is OK.

SPIRITUAL SMACKDOWN: YOU DON'T GET TO SKIP THE WORK

We hope that by now, for your own sanity, you've heard of the myth of the overnight success. If not, let us break it down for you: there's no such thing as an overnight success.

All so-called overnight successes are the result of many, many hours, weeks, months and years of hard work and determination, failures, successes and plateaus where nothing noteworthy happens either way, perseverance, belief and trying, trying and trying again. Then all of a sudden one day, a thousand pennies drop, the glass ceiling is broken, the deal is signed, the money flows in and their face is on TV and every must-read blog going. So it looks to everyone else like an overnight success, but that's only because it makes for a great romantic social media story and because all the hard work was going on, unseen, in the background.

A really smart guy named Malcolm Gladwell presented the theory in his awesome book, *Outliers,* that it takes around 10,000 hours of practice to become an expert in your field, whether it's your hobby, your passion or your profession. So let's say you work consistently on your thing for four hours a day – which is a lot for a hobby, and probably realistic for a work thing, bearing in mind breaks, distractions, meetings, e-mails, all the time we're not actually 'working' in a focused way on whatever it is – five days a week, every week. That's 500 days, or a little over 16 months to clock up your 10,000 hours.

So there's your practical 'real world' timeframe for becoming awesome at what you love, and what you're itching to be great at. Adjust the maths as you please based on whatever your thing is and how much time you have to dedicate to it. Then add on the spiritual work, i.e. all the emotional, psychic bumps in the road you're bound to hit if you're really doing your work in a conscious way. Those bumps that are delivered in the form of lessons you need to learn before you can really move forwards, and upper limits you'll no doubt hit as you make leaps and bounds in your development. Those bumps that give you the gift of a little extra awareness, the bumps that bump you right off course for months or years while you figure some big deal shit out, and the bumps that bump you onto a whole other course, when you realize this wasn't your thing after all.

Anything worth doing is gonna take some work, so you need to ask yourself are you willing to do that work, and stick with it until the light at the end of the tunnel becomes more than just a little glimmer in the distance? Everyone has to do it.

> ### Yes, you are special, but so is everyone else, so no, you don't get to skip the work.

Just because your feet are itching and your ego is future-tripping, you don't get to skip the work. Just because you've wanted this sooooo bad, since you were six years old, you don't get to skip the work. Just because everyone around you seems to be achieving what you want to achieve before you, doesn't mean you get to skip the work. Not if you really want what you say you want anyhow.

So buckle up and get ready for the ride. It won't always be pretty, it won't always be easy, it won't always be fun or exciting and when you're in it, it will feel like it's taking forever, but if you really want it you gotta turn your trust on and stay steady.

> ### Keep moving in the direction of your dreams because an inch forwards, even when it feels like two inches back (and trust us that the learning in those moments always leapfrogs you ahead later on) is better than standing still and complaining that it's taking too long, any day of the week.

DHARMA
NOT DOGMA

Finding your dharma is aligning with your soul's calling whether you receive money for it or not and, as John O' Donohue wrote in *Anam Cara: A Book of Celtic Wisdom*, 'Your soul knows the geography of your destiny. Your soul alone has the map of your future, therefore you can trust this indirect, oblique side of yourself.'

It is being and doing what you came here to do according to the divine order and the infinite wisdom of the Big U. The dictionary will back us up on this one: 'Dharma: The principle or law that orders the universe or the essential function or nature of a thing.'

For you, this may be retraining as an animal Reiki healer, starting a new tech company abroad or staying put and being the best goddamn dental receptionist the earth has ever seen.

Spoiler alert! If it makes you feel good, turns you on and lifts your spirit then that's a good indicator that you've found your calling or have at the very least unearthed some clues to it. Whether you turn that into a profession and source of income is entirely up to you.

In this section we want to help share some insights and ideas to shine a light on exploring making your dharma your day job as an option, as we're well aware there can be some stumbling blocks along the way. We've had the scraped knees and ripped jeans to prove it!

It feels like many of us are in danger of never knowing what it's like to live aligned with our dharma because of the dogma we're taught about how good girls and boys live their lives. Just so there's no confusion let's break it down: 'Dogma: A principle or set of principles laid down by an authority as incontrovertibly true.'

Is it just us or is the Universe totally conspicuous by its absence in that little definition?

Perhaps you had parents who told you only the sky was the limit or teachers that welcomed your debate and contradiction, or perhaps you've worked for a boss who just let you get on with it, trusting in your ideas and abilities – if so, you'll know how absolutely wonderful it is to have enjoyed unconditional support and freedom. You might also be aware that it's also not the norm. For many of us, while one of those champions may have been present, in other areas it's likely that 'should' took hold and became the dominant influence drowning out our dharma

Whether you are still undercover or a card-carrying, flag-waving lightworker, one of your first tasks out in the field will be to unpick the layers, assumptions and expectations that you've been led to believe are important and validate you, such as:

+ Having a 'good' or 'proper' job (whatever that is?!).

+ Knuckling down at school and getting good grades across the board (because in grown-up life you're totally expected to be an A student in ten completely different subjects… Not!!).

+ Not being 'greedy' or 'getting above your station'.

+ Being serious, concentrating and leaving daydreaming and play in the schoolyard.

+ Seeing a decision through and not changing direction, no matter how unaligned it feels. Nobody likes a flake!

+ Being nice.

+ Respecting authority and doing as you're told. (Even when it doesn't feel right.)

+ Waiting your turn.

+ Not expecting too much.

+ And preparing for the worst so you won't be disappointed.

It's easy to be swept along with any of the above because they're so widely perpetuated and accepted as truths in modern society. Though with the rising tide of lightworkers we're happy to see that things are slowly changing and generations of old-school dogmas are starting to be questioned more frequently and with more vigour – hello millennials!

That said, when we've lived with decades of conditioning in old-school dogmatic ways, it's easy to fall into *'shoulding'* all over ourselves if we're not careful. It's time to clean up, as this act of self-sabotage can severely affect our dharmic potential.

Follow your dharma, question the dogma

There's nothing to stress about and there's no shame attached to having 'gone with the flow' up 'til now, be that in your job, relationship, location or education. We're willing to bet our combined online shopping budget that there was no malice in the decisions you made because you thought you should – we can only do what we think is right at the time, based on the information we have. Part of the magic of life is that our true wisdom is revealed to us when we're ready and joyfully everything happens for a reason. For example:

✦ You chose to study finance, because that would make Mum and Dad proud, but you had no idea your love of animals would turn into a proper grown-up passion for conservation. And it turns out that degree in dollars would help you write a killer funding application for a snow leopard sanctuary.

- You did what felt like a thousand internships at architecture firms because your calling for energy healing was invisible to you, but later down the line your experience helped you design a centre for holistic healing for the homeless.

- You had parents that never showed any emotion, so you learnt to become an emotional detective and are now a kickass life coach because of all your early training.

- You were told tarot was black magic and 'for weirdos' but you decided to carry on regardless, while hustling at your day job, and now your run a thriving Facebook community for thousands of other 'weirdos' who needed your courage to pave the way and hold space for them.

If you chart it back, that niggling feeling of what you felt most aligned with never really stood a chance in the cold, ego-led, rational world you had been taught was the be all and end all. But thankfully the Big U had your back and made sure that whatever detours you took – or are currently taking along the way – would serve your dharma in some way, no matter how obscure.

Jo: Divinely designed

Before creating #HigherSelfie, before having my spiritual revelation and turning on a dime to become a spiritual life coach, I was a textile designer. I studied fashion and textiles for six years, right out of leaving school. I could have qualified as a doctor in that time, but I was convinced that all I ever wanted to be was a designer.

When the realization dawned on me that, yes, I was definitely a creative person but perhaps design wasn't destined to be my forever career path, there were a ton of difficult emotions to deal with. There was the shame and sense of failure that I felt around telling, (or for some time, avoiding telling) my parents after they'd paid for years of study. There was the sense of loss around letting go all I'd known and everything I'd committed my life and work to for as long as I could remember. And there was the fear that what I was stepping into was unknown. I didn't have a degree, let alone six years graft, in my new career path. Plus it had taken me six years to explain to my family what a textile designer was, so the thought of trying to explain 'spiritual life coach' was just... Ugh!

But I see now that throughout the different editions of my career, my design training and my first stab at running a business (and subsequently closing it down because it made no money!) served me well. I learned so much about business, about creativity, about marketing, branding and networking. Processes and overheads, deadlines and contracts. I learned that having a discerning eye for what looks good and why helps enormously when collaborating with others in business, and whenever I've needed to I could do anything design- or tech-related myself. Those hours and hours spent in a windowless CAD room at uni were not wasted on me!

So where do you start?

With the divine feminine rising and more and more lightworkers answering their individual clarion calls, times are quickly changing and we don't have time for you to wait. The world needs you in flow with your source energy now more than ever.

Practically speaking, getting aligned with your dharma might take some tiny tweaks in your overall outlook or it might mean a life overhaul – careers, relationships, body habits, the whole caboodle.

So it doesn't really matter *where* you start TBH – the trick is just to bloody start somewhere! Even if that's searching for your desired career path on Google or texting a friend to ask her to introduce you to someone that could help.

There are entire books written on the subject of how to find and live your purpose so we're not going to try and shoehorn in a generic plan that will serve as a fail-safe blueprint – not least because we all know there ain't nothing generic 'bout your dharma!

We opened with the advice that if it makes you feel good and lifts your spirit then it's probably a clue to your dharma and we urge you to act on that insight. The truth is:

Deep down we all know where and how we're meant be spending our time here on Earth, right now, but what with societal conditioning and ego's naughty tricks we can fall asleep and become unconscious to the truth, especially if it's not a 'normal' or well-worn path.

Luckily, your soul knows better than that and you could not be in safer hands. The fact you're even reading this book says something about your awareness level and that you're at a point of reflection and growth in your life.

As we demonstrated earlier, the timing of your life is always perfect and your spiritual GPS will always make sure you're on the right course for where you're at in life, helping you to pick up skills and lessons that will be useful somewhere along the way. So you really can start doing your dharma whenever you're ready, but we strongly suggest, with the support of a whole tribe of #HigherSelfie brothers and sisters out there reading and being fired up by these same words at this exact moment, that you start today.

Waking up spiritually is age-, background- and gender-neutral, and no matter when, where or how you do it, the experience of a higher state of consciousness will always throw up questions about your current reality and how you transition to a more consistently aligned life.

This self-questioning will challenge you to think twice about your view of the world and how it works. It's an opportunity to invite Spirit to take the wheel while your ego takes a time-out!

Engaging fully in this invitation of discovery will allow you truly to free your soul and wake up your life. However, it doesn't always feel easy as we stumble over questions such as 'Why did it take so long for me to get here?', 'How do I move forwards?', 'What should I do now?', 'Has my whole career so far been a waste of time?', 'Is my boyfriend a useless bum slowing me down?' or 'Should I cash in all my belongings, move to an ashram and go vegan even though I love bacon and reading *Vogue*?!'

Slow down there, speedy spirit lover! You have time to figure it all out in a way that feels authentic to you, on your own terms.

Nothing thus far in your life has been a mistake. It's all been part of your divine assignment and it's down to you to accept and receive that universal truth, and use the insight to help you get in the dharmic vortex.

Your dharma lounge – VIP entry only

Once you open up to living your dharma and letting the universal flow of energy be present in how you live your life – especially how you choose to be of service, it's important to apply the principles of self-preservation to your dream and vision. As you manifest your dharma into reality you might be called to keep it free from the interfering eyes of others who might not understand it, until you feel steady on your feet and ready to show yourself to the world. Trust that. Yogi Bhajan said 'There's nothing which can be more precious in you than your own relationship with your own consciousness.'

Lucy: To have and to hold, honour and protect...

When Jo and I created the concept of #HigherSelfie it would have been so easy to share it around with all and sundry right then and there. The nugget of the idea alone felt electric and we knew it was divine guidance. We could have posted it on Facebook, shouted it over the loud bar music to friends, texted every person we ever knew to share our exciting idea about the event, and just get it out there in any and every digital and real-life way. But it didn't feel right – we knew we had to honour the idea, protect it, nurture it and feed it so it could show itself to us fully and we could do the very best job of bringing it to life. So even though we were so excited that our conversations bubbled over into hours of chatting and creation that turned into huge to-do lists, and we obsessively texted each other about it, it stayed between the two of us in a VIP lounge with invitation-only exclusive entry, and for a long time we were the only two on the list.

Your dream deserves sacred secret status whilst it reveals itself to you.

A process of becoming

Finding your dharma is a process of becoming. The process is sensitive and sacred, to be revered and respected, and it deserves special VIP treatment and the space necessary to receive all of the potential wonder and guidance that comes with tuning in to your soul's desire.

You are the best-qualified, capable and deserving candidate for all of the gifts that you'll discover on your journey of realignment.

It's helpful to be aware that along the way outside sources may try and suggest or even convince you to the contrary…

'I don't wanna sound like a Debby Downer but…'

'I'm just being a realist, mate, c'mon…'

'It's nothing to do with me but do you really know what you're doing?'

'Aren't you getting a bit ahead of yourself, I mean, what if...?'

Unsolicited advice and comments like this totally suck!

As you wake up your life and free your soul, by getting and staying in flow with the Universe, you are bound to encounter some, ahem, 'feedback' on any changes you make that take you in a new direction. They might come from your own ego *or* the egos of your friends and family. Double joy!

It's more than likely that people are going to question your reasons and share some hideous anecdote about someone they knew who did what you were planning to do and they ended up in a Thai jail or flat broke and living in the YMCA.

As well-meaning as they may be in handing out their advice, it is not necessarily going to be helpful or serve your bigger vision for yourself to hear it or be around it. If taken to heart, it will at best delay your decision to follow your dharma, and at worst convince you it was a crazy idea in the first place and you should probably just get back to reality, cosy down with ego and let him remind you that not everyone is lucky enough to be able to follow their dreams.

Hear this, sweet cheeks: You need to shut that mutherfluffer down immediately!

You need to become zero tolerance with anyone who trash-talks your dream.

And yup, we've even got a loving solution for that. Our fave angel whisperer Doreen Virtue uses the affirmation 'Cancel, clear, delete' to close the metaphorical glass doors on other people's crap talk about your dharma.

Whenever you're subjected to someone's less than supportive unsolicited opinion on what you're up to, just smile and repeat the affirmation, 'Cancel, clear, delete' in your mind, then when they've finished, move swiftly on to where you're going for lunch, or how you have to dash for your bus.

Your dharma lounge needs to become an invitation-only area exclusively for you and your vision until you are ready to invite in the people that can support you, either by helping you out or simply just being there.

Dr Wayne Dyer spelled this out clearly in *Wishes Fulfilled*, his guide to manifesting:

> *You must be adamant that your imagination*
> *is your sacred private space… It is an*
> *inner sanctum you share with the creative*
> *source of the universe… Place no limits*
> *on what you are allowed to imagine*
> *and put up a 'keep out' sign to protect*
> *the space… Invite the unseen world*
> *of spirit to come in and guide you.*

This is of the highest importance because once you own it and commit to it, the energy attached to your dharma exponentially multiplies and the Universe can guide you divinely on your own path of discovery.

Build a bridge and get over it

Most people we know on the spiritual scene have bridged to being full-time in their passion business over a few years.

It has taken graft, working for free, swapping favours, training, investment, commitment and hustle to get to the full-time, lifestyle-supporting, gonna take a two-week-vacation-now-and-pay-for-it-in-full level. It's authenticity, belief and focus that have brought them the fame, the clients, the book deals and abundant life.

But if you go by social media posts alone or other people's spin you could be forgiven for thinking that one day they left their job and the next day they created a successful dharma-led business and lifestyle, faster than you can get into your down dog. Like there was no in-between stage and they just simply manifested themselves an awesome life and career and 'abracadabra!' their lives were transformed!

For some, going 'all in' and using their life savings to leave one career and start another, without transition, is their path. They've made the decision, bought the course, had the 'no obligation discovery call', done the affirmations and are going to work full-time hustling to find clients (that, by the way, are never just waiting there) and commit it all to that one business. There are some very successful teachers that follow that business model themselves and advocate it to their clients who, in turn, go all in and throw the kitchen sink at it and they are seemingly very successful.

If it works for you, go for it! We're all about adapting the rhetoric to what you know in your soul works for you. Zero judgement if you're more of a bridge burner than a bridge builder and it's served you well.

What we're not so keen on is the hard sell, double-or-quits tone of some of the conversations out there that imply if you don't put it all on the line – your savings, your mortgage, your relationship, your time – then you're somehow confusing the Universe or that you're not fully committed to your dream.

We're walking, talking proof that the opposite is true so we invite you to consider the possibility of a 'bridging period' to get you from where you are to where you want to be.

It almost seems silly to feel called to defend (watch out ego!) this as a route to a dream, but bridge jobs get so much bad press that we want to smash the taboo.

In the lead up to where the #HigherSelfie brand is now we both did other paying work outside of the business. Those other jobs did not stop us writing the book you're currently holding, putting on sold-out workshops, securing significant investment from global brand sponsors, featuring in the national press, putting on one of the biggest wellbeing events the UK has ever seen with our un-conference and the list could go on!

Our bridge jobs did exactly as they were intended to: transition us towards our true calling and living in flow. They have contributed to our #HigherSelfie dream, not taken away from it. Having our bills covered meant that we could sleep at night. We don't know about you, but we continue to function – and serve our clients and community – best on a full night's sleep and zero anxiety about the rent being due!

Plus knowing a bridge job is temporary is tremendously empowering, as even on a tough day it's just another eight hours chalked off towards your bigger picture.

Back then we chose roles where we knew exactly what was needed from us – no grey areas, very little overtime (unless we wanted it), flexible hours and time off in lieu if we needed it – which kept our energy levels up and meant we could fully, and with love, deliver for our employers at the time and our business.

In our bridge jobs we didn't really have to work weekends so we actually got some rest, some time to spend with our families, go to friends' weddings, y'know the stuff you really don't want to miss, and recharge our creative stores for what #HigherSelfie and its Big Magic asked of us.

This period of splitting our working weeks encouraged us to focus and prioritize our efforts and made us super-efficient with how we used our time outside of employed work. When you only have two days a week to do your dharma, you'd better bet they'll be the most high-octane, high-vibe and productive work days of your life!

In order to reach the ideal bridging phase, we both left organizations and roles that we felt weren't allowing us to be authentic, that we knew we could no longer fully deliver for under the conditions and that were draining us, whether that was through tyrannical politics and hard-to-handle characters or quite literally from lifting and carrying all day. Those jobs left us doubting ourselves and too weak to show up mentally or physically for our dream.

Don't get it twisted, a bridge job does not mean avoiding what's expected from you by your boss or team. We absolutely do not promote skiving, being dishonest or burdening your teammates with the work you were too distracted to do – if you're employed to do a job, do the job! A bridge job should be a conscious and responsible choice that allows you to give, without your energy, time, effort and creativity feeling like they're being taken from you without your consent.

Welcome to Dharma-ville! First exit over the bridge…

You must check in with what's true for you when it comes to the support you need right now. Your current job may not be your bridge job and only you will know how long you can continue with the status quo.

We knew individually, before we had even met each other, that the Big U had plans for us even if we had no idea what they were. With strong faith in that knowing, it was clear that our job situations at the time were not conducive to the growth we wanted to pursue to fulfil our dharmic callings.

For Lucy, working in an advertising agency, the long hours were exhausting, the pressure was intense and unrelenting, and difficult personalities and politics were at the darker times making her feel insecure, apathetic and miserable.

For Jo, working in social media roles for successful wellbeing pros took her focus and time away from her love of following and teaching *ACIM*, which was making her feel frustrated, inauthentic and as though she was wasting her gifts.

At those times, pre-bridge jobs, the urge to scratch the itch of our respective callings was so strong we knew we couldn't wait and had to course-correct ASAP. Even if seeking alternative employment just bought us some time to recover and think about what we really wanted for ourselves, we each knew it would be of value to serve our respective dharmas.

And so it was we were able, in our own different ways, to understand what we truly needed in terms of money coming in and free time to bridge to doing our dharma, full-time. Our lists were pretty similar even though we didn't know each other at the time. The non-negotiables went a bit like this:

+ Working with and for people we liked and respected

+ Pays X amount of cash per month.

+ Non-political vibe in the workplace (because navigating that minefield is a whole other job in itself, which is even more exhausting than the actual job and for which you receive zero cash!).

+ A 9 to 5 role that would mean we had our evenings and weekends free to choose to spend working on our dharma or taking some well-earned time off.

+ Straightforward working processes that did not necessitate reporting in to lots of people and would allow us to utilize the skills we already had.

+ Preferably in a creative organization.

+ A maximum one-hour commute (or much, much less for Jo – you can take the girl out of the provinces…).

We were happy to bridge to our dream. Working in service of our dharma *and* getting a pay cheque was always going to be a good idea even if we were serving drinks or writing sales presentations!

So over to you…

+ What do you want/need to earn per month to feel supported?

+ Where can you get the money you need on the terms you desire?

+ What boxes do you need to tick in terms of criteria for an ideal bridge job?

+ How long can you realistically stand to stay where you are right now? And at what cost to your energy, outlook and self-esteem?

Follow your light to Google, discover your bridge and find some of the answers you need, right away, to get a plan together.

You are hereby called to move from dogma to dharma and be irritatingly persistent in the pursuit of your soul's growth.

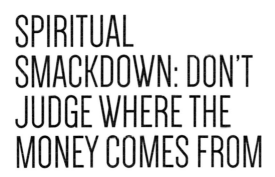

SPIRITUAL SMACKDOWN: DON'T JUDGE WHERE THE MONEY COMES FROM

A little disclaimer before we begin this spiritual spanking (Ooh! Saucy!) We're not suggesting you join a criminal gang, start selling stuff that 'fell off the back of a truck' or stealing money from your mum's purse!

What we are suggesting is that when you need a financial income, which if you're an independent adult living on the grid in the 21st century, is going to be always, that you don't start laying judgements on whether that money is legit, whether you're worthy of it or deserve it depending on its source.

If you've been down on your knees praying for help to claw back some time and energy to spend on your passion project, and your partner who's doing well in their super-steady job offers to cover the rent for six months while you take a career break to work full-time on your side-hustle, take it that the call has been answered and this is a gift you should openly and gratefully accept.

If you've set up an Etsy shop selling cute prints and awesome sweatshirts and your ten best customers are your mates and your cool aunty, that's legit. You have a business and people are buying your stuff. A lot of super-successful businesses start out selling their wares to people they know – in some circles that's called networking!

If your friend who has a healthy chunk of cash saved up for a house deposit but can't find anywhere they love, so has called off the search for a year or two, offers to loan you the money to build your new website, like right away, take it, you crazy!

If you're in need of financial support, drop your judgement about where it comes from. There's no shame in accepting a leg-up from friends and loved ones. You're not a daddy's girl or a loser or an embarrassment if you didn't 'earn' the money that is currently keeping a roof over your head.

There'll be plenty of time for hustling your arse off and earning your keep when you're waist-deep in your dharma, so what are you waiting for? Say yes to the Universe's offer of divine compensation. You're worth every penny ;-)

BEWARE OF
THE TROLLS

Trolling, that is, throwing insults, provocations, threats and general emotional slime, seems like a thoroughly modern phenomenon but it's actually been going on for as long as humans have been gossiping about and judging each other.

It's just that in this digital age, it's sooo much easier for trolls to seek out their victims and for those unfortunate enough to be on the receiving end of it to see, hear and read what these mean-spirited critics have to say. We've swapped the mudslinging round the campfire for blog pages dedicated to sarcastic memes, bitchy comments and, in its most extreme form, cyber bullying, stalking and harassment.

Remember how we talked about 'out-spiriting' coming from a fear of separation (*see page 16*)? Trolling comes from the exact same shadowy place too.

It's a belief that talking shit about someone else raises the troll up, rather than the truth: it's simply a reflection of their own fears. Their fear of not being good enough, pretty enough, talented enough, funny enough, smart enough or brave enough to put their own selves out on the line… Or even quite literally, online.

*It is not the critic who counts; not the man who
points out how the strong man stumbles, or where
the doer of deeds could have done them better.
The credit belongs to the man who is actually in
the arena, whose face is marred by dust and sweat
and blood… who at best knows in the end the
triumph of high achievement, and who at the worst,
if he fails, at least fails while daring greatly…*

THE MAN IN THE ARENA, THEODORE ROOSEVELT

As a creative person – and anyone who makes something that didn't exist before they touched it is creative – when you express yourself you're being vulnerable and putting yourself out into the arena. Hopefully you'll manage to avoid the blood part from the quote above, but the sweat, tears and dust storm that what you create kicks up might well be in abundance just by you being you.

To quote one of our all time faves Brené Brown in her 99U talk from 2013 '…if you're going to show up and be seen, there is only one guarantee, and that is, you are going to get your ass kicked…'

In that keynote Brené is talking about stepping out into the arena, and showing yourself fully, whatever that is for you – a new job, writing a blog, coming out, working on your relationship or speaking your woo-woo, angel-loving truth. When you choose to be brave and authentic and put yourself, your passion, your work out into the world people will have something to say about it, and sadly it isn't always going to be 'Well done!' accompanied by a friendly pat on the back.

You can either be judged or you can be ignored

It would be lovely if everyone listened to that old favourite saying of mums everywhere 'if you have nothing nice to say, don't say anything at all.' Unfortunately it doesn't work that way and sharp words can hit us from all directions, especially in the online world where it's easy to hide behind a handle and an avatar. For the most part trolls never have to face up to the consequences of their actions.

Jo: Time for a new hobby...

I once read a troll's personal story in a magazine. She was a young woman in her twenties and admitted being dissatisfied in an underpaid job where her boss disrespected her. She wanted a relationship but felt she couldn't 'get one'. So in her spare time she trolled Twitter, anonymously, as a hobby. In fact she'd said such offensive things to some celebrities that she'd had her account shut down, only to reopen another under a different name. She said in the article that when she was happier, when she had a better job and a boyfriend she'd stop trolling.

Now I know this is not the profile of everyone that has ever trolled. Some people are genuinely convinced of their personal vendetta and feel they have a legitimate right to throw insults, accusations and knife, gun and bomb emojis around on the Internet, but doesn't it demonstrate how deep this fear of separation goes, and how it can drive some really unhealthy behaviour? Not to mention the bitter irony of someone who basically insults and hurts people for a hobby thinking that other areas of their life will make positive shifts while their energy is so off – and let's face it, pretty gross – in their spare time.

If you do come up against unsolicited, unpleasant feedback online, whether that's passive-aggressive guidance or just straight-up nasty comments, the best thing to do is cut off the oxygen to the situation. Block that person, report their account and use your spiritual practice to help you move onwards and upwards. It just isn't worth the energy to allow unhappy strangers to limit how your light shines, on- or offline.

Some people, including us, would say that if you're dividing opinion then you are doing something right, so keep on keeping on safe in the knowledge the Universe has your back and that you are being called to step into your power despite the weird behaviour of those faceless, cowardly souls who trawl the Internet looking for their next victim.

Up close, personal and a pain in the arse

Being trolled online by randoms happens more than you might think – you just have to look at the comments section of any YouTube video to back that up (and quite frankly for a good LOL, if you find dodgy spelling, bad grammar and really tenuous points hilarious, as we do!) Yet sometimes, someone makes a point of getting in your face and picking you out for a cup of their spooially brewed extra-cold mean juice.

Lucy: It isn't all unicorns and rose quartz

Being involved with something like #HigherSelfie has led to some mega high-vibe online connections and friendships. We're often overwhelmed with the support and love we get online, always doing our best to reply personally and with emojis, obvs. But it isn't all unicorns and rose quartz unfortunately, and there was an incident where someone singled me out on social media and over a series of Instagram posts and e-mails to important people in our business. They, for want of a better term, came after me. They used really gross, highly inappropriate language to try and insult me personally, but worse than this they called into question our love of Khloe Kardashian and use of mermaid artwork in our communications. I'll be honest, for about five seconds the knife, bomb and gun emojis did shake me up as I'd never experienced this kind of callous vitriol before, but on sharing what was happening with people that I trust, I received such a gorgeous outpouring of support that I immediately knew this was just part of my assignment from the Universe. Plus Big U also created lawyers for when this kind of thing starts to get out of hand! Thank you Universe! LOL #butseriously

Haters gon' hate!

It almost seems crazy to care about someone you don't know saying something irrelevant about you on the Internet – something we can tune in or out of as we choose, but being judged or criticized so openly, so harshly and by so many sure does take a strong stomach and a steady soul. It would be remiss not to share the golden advice we received from our buddies when we came up against the heat of online hate...

'Forgive and delete' is a favourite of Gabby B's and if anything is going to cut through that negative crap it's incinerating the impulse to react and get dragged into a battle. Get a system. This was recommended by our friend Emma Lloyd and has served us so well. A 'go to' strategy in sticky situations is helpful because if you know what to do it can bring clarity of purpose in the moment. You could even go as far as to create an actual document to refer to that goes a bit like this:

Start off with a statement of your purpose and intention, then an acknowledgement that not everyone in the world will see it (too bad for them!). Then list what actions you can take, for example:

+ Block, delete or report.

+ Don't engage with the trolls.

+ Say a prayer or whatever ritual works for you.

+ Do some self-care.

+ Review the positive things people have said about your work (it's not big-headed or vain to keep a file of these).

+ Ask folks around you not to tell you if they see this stuff – it's not helpful.

+ When you're feeling clearer and safer, review which bits of what the trolls said really niggled you and have a think about whether you share any of these views (it sounds counterintuitive but sometimes when people say things that echo our darkest fears it can trigger us) and decide if there's anything you want to do differently – or not.

✦ Have a cocktail/cup of tea/ beer and toast your own growth, light and magnificence!

Having a system for icky stuff like this is awesome because when emotions are running high you need something to ground you. It's like practising your evacuation route in case of a fire because the last thing you want to be doing when shit gets real is running round like a headless chicken, being all irrational and reactive in your rush to make it stop or protect yourself.

And take our word for it, even knowing you have the back-up of a system strengthens your resolve to stay in the arena and keep showing up for your dream.

Unpopular opinion: When trolling happens across the dinner table

Unfortunately criticism, judgement and negative comments are not limited to our online lives and can come at us when we're face to face with people that we would like to think are on our team. Friends, family, partners, lovers, workmates, acquaintances, bosses and in-laws can sometimes make their sceptical feelings known in a less than tactful way that totally pops the balloon of positivity we're holding.

It's bad enough when you're getting advice from your dad about whatever field he's an expert in, but it starts to get really crazy-making when your nearest and dearest haven't got the faintest idea what they're even commenting on. Who would have thought people would have so much to say about something they know so little about?

Criticism or withheld support from those we care about can be the most difficult to ignore and the hardest to accept, especially when we are striving to live consciously and grow and just y'know, be good people.

It can often feel like it comes out of nowhere, via side eye glances, ignoring whole swathes of your update e-mail, or robotic nodding as you describe what you're up to, followed by swiftly changing the subject. This passive dissent can make us feel the most wobbly. After all, if those that are supposed to love us unconditionally can't get behind us, what chance do we have?

It's important here to get super-mindful that you are not your actions, words or deeds and your soul and the core of who you are are not in question. Sometimes we have to be our own cheerleader when it comes to our passion project, life choices or change of direction in order to make up the fist pumps and whoop whoops that we'd hope would come from those in our close circle.

Criticism or silent judgement of our ideas, dreams or progress by others is part of our earthly assignment and not everyone is going to be super-enthusiastic about the calls you decide to make for yourself *and* it goes both ways. C'mon, we've all exclaimed the odd silent 'WTF?' on hearing about a friend dumping her seemingly perfect boyfriend out of nowhere when she's been pining for a committed relationship for years. (Google Aidan and Carrie in *SATC* for the ultimate reminder of that scenario!)

We've all done it and we've all received it too, but when we're in the latter position, it calls for some stella-strength self-care and focus to stay on your chosen unicorn and see through your ideas even if Mum raises her eyebrows, your BFF thinks you're bonkers or your partner makes jokes about your idea in public. (Just remember, cancel, clear, delete!)

And if you're in need of neat verbal shut-down you're welcome to use our default response when we sense the negative judgement coming on; 'It works for me.' That cuts the comment off at the knees and stops it having to become a discussion where you can fall into the trap of justifying. It also builds space around you so that you can stand strong in your belief and not feel you have to provide any more content for them to criticize. Then continue on your merry way and really give them something to talk about, as you shine your light even brighter.

FORGIVENESS: 'I'M LIKE, SO SORRY'

The 'F' word is one of such a swelling significance that it bears setting some ground to help anchor it in our modern perception.

We love a definition that we heard from Oprah: 'Forgiveness is giving up on the hope it could ever have been any different.'

We also believe that forgiveness is a gift we give ourselves. Forgiveness is not something that is a 'hall pass' or 'glossing over' the pain that an act or experience may have caused you. Forgiveness isn't about letting someone or something 'off the hook', it's about setting yourself free from the pain, anguish and bitterness that holding a grudge causes.

In terms of your spiritual workout, forgiveness feels like one of the heaviest emotional, soul-level workouts, but like doing double Zumba on a Saturday morning with a hangover, once you've done it you'll be lighter, faster, stronger and a shit ton more kickass for it. More than this, you'll thank yourself.

We say 'once you've done it' but to be clear, it's defo not just a one time and it's done kinda thing (because if it was everyone would already be doing it!). Like all spiritual practices, through a continued and conscious flow of awareness, love and inspired action, you can experience forgiveness.

You only have to look at the news to know that forgiveness is not something to be taken lightly or thought of as a one-off fix. The modern world, and especially the current rising-up of the collective ego – manifested in war, violence and destruction – is an assault on our individual Spirits and our global consciousness.

Exposing the darkness

If we think of the ego as darkness and our Spirit or connection to the Universe as light, the only way to diminish or even completely get rid of the ego is to shine light on it. You cannot crush or sweep away or KO darkness, you can only turn on the light.

As the collective consciousness shifts and gets stronger and modern lightworkers (that's you!) rise up with the insatiable feeling inside that something must change, that there must be a better way, the ego fears its own death. Fear after all, is its speciality! So the collective ego begins to rise up and get stronger in defence.

That's why we seem to be experiencing an unparalleled level of death, destruction and dishonesty around the world. Yet equally, historic abuses and untruths are uncovered daily and ethical cooperatives, volunteer groups, activists and holistic healers of all modalities are swelling in their numbers. Everywhere that darkness is hiding, the light is seeking it out.

No longer can anyone hide – no matter the size of the company, country or military might they stand behind, no matter their 'position' in the human hierarchy. Where darkness has remained hidden for decades and centuries it is now being exposed to the light.

Forgiveness needs to become part of our regular repertoire, if we are to be able to survive the onslaught of what the collective ego has to throw at us.

It begins within

As with all spiritual activism it must begin at home, within every one of us, within our own minds and our thoughts about ourselves. Often the person we forget to forgive most often, yet whom we need to work on forgiving most generously, is ourself.

Whenever we forgive we induce a miracle, because a miracle is a change in perception. So where we have judged ourselves, made ourselves bad or wrong, we change the perception. We see ourselves as innocent children, simply misguided in a moment of ego, and we return to love. *Voila*! Miracle!

As with all miracles there is no order of difficulty. So forgiving yourself when you feel guilty for taking a night off for a Netflix binge instead of working on your latest passion purpose project, is just as valid and required an act as forgiving that guy that cheated on you, or sending love to faraway lands and people we see in the brutal news stories on our Twitter feeds each morning.

Lucy: No shortcuts

I used to have a really bad gossip problem – actually let's call it an addiction. Before I heard the cosmic alarm clock, I used to pit myself against other people all the time and have an underlying sense of competition that I am now pleased to say has left the building! But a few years ago, if I was jealous of what somebody was doing or achieving then I would immediately engage in a bitchy conversation about it, whether it was ranting to a friend via a text message or talking behind their back in a nightclub bathroom at 3 a.m. I was so insecure that I had to recruit others into my bitchy gossipy ways, as a thinly veiled attempt to cover up that it was all coming from me and I just couldn't help myself. It was something I grew to be really ashamed and anxious about. I used to lie awake at night beating myself up for being such a bitter, horrible person but at the same time having evil thoughts about the people I was bitching about like, 'I really hope his girlfriend cheats on him... If he isn't with me then screw his happiness!' or 'I hope she messes up that presentation at work – she's so full of herself' and 'I hope she puts all that weight back on, then let's see if she can get a boyfriend!'

I thought this was just a personality trait and a part of who I was and, for that reason, I was stuck with it. A tendency to be bitchy, sly and hurtful here and there was 'my thing', right? It became increasingly clear once I had heard the cosmic alarm clock that this was *not* the case.

Yet rather than jump for joy at my clean slate in the acknowledgment that I could be a supportive, easy-going person and not talk whack about people, I suffered an enormous guilt hangover for all the bad energy I had created and the crappy attitude I'd promoted. I was completely lost in guilt and wanted so desperately to make amends and go back in time and just *be* different. I wrote imaginary letters of apology in my head.

Dear <insert bitching victim here>, You probably don't remember me but I used to roll my eyes when you spoke in social situations and openly criticize you in front of our friends. I'm so sorry I disrespected you... And um, yeah, sorry about that even though you had no idea... Umm byeeee! Love, Lucy

Seems heavy, right? Having to forgive myself for some nasty conversations that the person in question never really knew about? But the forgiveness isn't what's heavy. It's the guilt we lay on ourselves for not constantly being up to scratch in every way.

You might be reading this and thinking 'But why on earth did you feel guilty, you turned it all around. You shouldn't feel guilty!' And you're right! In theory, I *know* this. If you told me the same story about you, I'd tell you the same thing: there's no shame in trying to right a wrong. In fact it's an important part of being a responsible adult.

But it's been a while (like never!) since I was mistaken for Moses on the mountaintop, so yeah, sometimes my ego kicks in and I feel guilty for it. But thankfully I practise what I preach (most of the time!) and I was able to work a miracle by forgiving myself, or shining a light on the ego's darkness and changing my perception.

Today as I write this, I know in retrospect that my soul needed that embarrassing behaviour for its growth. There could be no shortcut if I was to be the woman I am evolving to be today. And the same goes for the anecdotes you have about mistakes or regrets you harbour from your own past, whether it was just last week, or when you were 12 years old in the playground.

Dear Ex, I forgive you!

So hopefully now you can now see how the shadow can help deliver you to light. But what about the *really* difficult ones? Like the exes, the work colleagues and, hold the phone, your parents?

If you want to live a life free of the sort of insidious bitterness that makes you all kinds of ill, and free of the kind of just-floating-beneath-the-surface frustration that is exhausting and makes you less than a joy to be around, you've got to go to work consciously on your most difficult relationships.

Jo: The unexpected ripple

In my private coaching practice I've seen the unexpected ripple effect of miracles that happen when you work on forgiving deep, long-held grievances. I've seen a client forgive her father for childhood misdeeds, which freed up a ton of other emotional weight she was carrying and was holding her back in her business. She focused her spiritual attention on forgiving her dad and not only did she come out with a better relationship with all of her extended family and a much improved sense of self-worth, but abundance began pouring into her business.

And in my own life I've experienced untold miracles inspired by forgiveness. After the end of a particularly intense and dysfunctional relationship, I did some heavy lifting on letting go of him, it and everything we had future-tripped into. I had profound spiritual experiences in meditation, including being visited by someone who had recently passed on, who, of course, knew everything was going just as it should and was smiling down on the whole situation.

Although in the mortal realm the pain and grief of loss was still there, it got miles better every day, so much weight was lifted. Even though I was still sad about the end of the relationship and recalibrating what the mechanics of my life looked and felt like, I understood on a deep soul level that this was all meant to happen, and why it was happening. All of these unexpected ripples from my forgiveness work resulted in me being clear enough of mind and spirit to hear the message that told me my life purpose. So not only was I able to move through the pain of the end of a relationship with grace and pace, but my whole life changed when I handed over the most difficult situation in my life at the time and opened up to there being a different, better plan.

We hope the benefit of working those forgiveness muscles is starting to outweigh any resistance to this sometime creaky-feeling concept ('But I don't wanna!' LOL! We've all been there!), and the gifts it can offer you are becoming clear.

Forgiveness, proper

Real humble, loving, vulnerable forgiveness is powerful. We don't mean any of that 'holier than thou' God complex crap – i.e. 'I'm forgiving you because I'm so enlightened and you, mere mortal, know not what you do.' Rather 'I'm forgiving you because I too have hurt people before, I too have made mistakes and I too would like to be loved and forgiven, so I'm offering you the same courtesy with grace and humility.'

ACIM teaches that only what you are not giving can be lacking in any situation, ergo if you would like to be loved and forgiven and treated with compassion you must seek out the ways you can find the compassion for others, even if they have hurt you.

Jo: Lessons in forgiveness

Two of the most valuable lessons I ever learned about forgiveness come from my all-time fave spiritual teacher Marianne Williamson. I'm obsessed with Marianne's audio lectures and have listened to them many, many times while walking my dogs or sitting in trains, planes and automobiles.

The first is that 'forgiveness doesn't mean you have to take them out to lunch!' Forgiveness doesn't mean that what they did was OK, or that whoops, you meditated on it and look it's all rosy and you're BFFs again. In this particular lecture she quoted Martin Luther King Jr. as saying, 'I'm so glad God said I must love my enemies because that means I don't have to like them.' It's like that commonly used defence of free speech: 'I don't agree with what you say but I defend your right to say it.'

Instead of suddenly having to become best friends with the person you can choose this wonderful thing called self-preservation instead. What that looks like is 'I send love and high vibes to you, I forgive, I wish you only the highest good and I won't be taking your calls, kind regards.'

The other lesson is that it's OK to have a moment of hurt. Again, being 'spiritual' doesn't mean that you are some freaky positivity robot that wears a perma-smile and can always immediately see the good in every person and situation.

ACIM says that you – *the real you* (not the one in the human suit wrapped up in break-room drama, *Mad Men* and WhatsApp group gossip!) cannot be hurt.

But this body and brain we got dealt sure is capable of feeling pain and upset and offence and it's super-important for your health that you *feel* those emotions. Sometimes you need to let yourself have a night of feeling pissed off and eating ice cream, or throwing darts at a picture of their face (LOLZ! We won't judge!) *before* you can go to work on the forgiveness piece.

If it's a much deeper trauma then you absolutely must allow yourself the time and grace to process the hurt properly, with help if required, before trying to skip a step and jump straight to forgiveness for the sake of 'being spiritual'.

There's nothing spiritual about false forgiveness, under which bubbles an ever-festering pot of hate, bitterness, guilt, shame and resentment. There's something distinctly unsettling about the yoga teacher in her organic cotton tee and vegan nail polish, proclaiming to have a great relationship with her ex, sipping her green juice through gritted teeth, with a cricked neck from the sheer effort it's taking to hold in her true vitriol. Even Louise Hay punches pillows on her bed! #justsayin

Get a little distance

A really effective part of that magic trick we call self-preservation, otherwise known as boundaries, self-care or putting your own oxygen mask on first is getting distance, physically and emotionally, from a situation that is driving you cray cray.

The physical aspect we've covered. So not only is lunch off the cards but you can also stop calling/taking their calls/e-mailing them/replying to their messages/commenting and liking their Facebook posts or Instagram feed.

If you know that physical distance is what you really need for the good of your own health, commit to it. Stop coming up with great excuses to self-sabotage and let that sucky energy – whether it's yours or theirs – leak in, because the discomfort is familiar and you're feeling sorry for yourself right now.

Treat yourself with the respect you deserve if you know it's right. An amazing book called *It's Called a Break Up Because It's Broken* by husband-and-wife relationship tag team Greg Behrendt and Amiira Ruotola Behrendt suggests 60 unbroken days of no contact to help heal the painful pull of wanting or needing to get in touch with someone you've broken up with. They're talking about romantic relationships, but we'd say this solid guideline is failsafe for all situations from you need some healing distance.

And yes, you need to feel into what's right for you, but if you're looking for a place to start that 60-day rule is a pretty awesome one. You can always reassess after 60 days, but our guess is you'll be in a very different place by then, and so will they.

But what about the emotional side? How do you get emotional distance from a painful situation when it lives inside your head and your brain obsessively plays it over and over?!

Like all the most effective solutions it's frustratingly simple... but ego likes to keep us stuck, small and safe, so one of its tricks is helping to convince you that nothing could be 'that easy' or 'that simple'.

Like reining in your debt couldn't be as simple as calling the credit card companies, setting up payment plans and cutting up the cards so you can't spend on them any more. No, no, you're going to have to do some intensive work on your wealth consciousness (and that would totes help you get to the root of the problem, but not if it's just a snazzy avoidance technique) for which you'll need to ahem, purchase an expensive seminar ticket on said credit cards and, oooh, did I see new season shoes?!

Like not talking to your ex could be as simple as deleting their number, not picking up their calls and deleting their drunken texts before reading. Nooo, it couldn't possibly be!

Like returning back to centre could be as simple as taking five minutes out in the loo at work to meditate and breathe. That's just crazy talk. As if!!

Hold up. Nine times out of ten, it really is that simple.

It's a symptom of the society we live in that doing something that's good and healthy and helpful for ourselves is always the hardest thing to do. We're not taught self-love as a default and everything we've described above are examples of acts of true self-love. So how do you employ this awareness when it comes to getting some emotional space between you and whatever or whomever you're working on forgiving? You pray.

Prayer

Prayer – or 'asking' as it's otherwise known, for the spiritually nervous – is the fast-track fix to giving you emotional distance in a difficult situation. If you feel you've been wronged, ask for help soothing your wounds. Ask for help seeing the truth of the other person, not just their misguided behaviour. Ask for the highest good for them, for you and for the whole situation.

If you're the one who messed up, do the same, just flip it. Ask for forgiveness, ask for healing for the other person, ask to see yourself as, and to act like, the person you really are, not the version who's currently sitting head down on the naughty step because she was mean to her friend. Ask for the highest good for all concerned. Be willing to admit your part in it – no exceptions – and ask to be shown the best course of action so that everyone can move through it.

Pray for five minutes every day for 30 days – seeing as we're getting all technical and shiz in this chapter – and see how much space you've created between you and the monkey that previously resided on your back, in just a month's time.

Cut those cords and delete their number

We know it can feel difficult in a world of constant connection, where the term 'unfriending' provokes a sharp intake of breath and gossip magazines chart the incessant following and unfollowing of Instagram accounts by celebrities who are on-again-off-again, but at the time of writing there are approximately 6,999,999,999 other people in the world just waiting to meet you/be your friend/future husband or wife/ business partner/dancing buddy, so you've no need to be lonely.

Plus you've always, always, got you and the Universe. So yeah you might miss them/it, but if cutting contact aids your recovery (and it probably will) you're not missing out.

So if your situation calls for some intense inner healing, free of the complications of constant, or even just sporadic, contact, follow these steps:

+ Delete their number, and e-mail, block their Facebook account. Yes we said block. Unfollow on Twitter, Instagram and Pinterest and wherever other social accounts connect you to them.

+ Delete all your old e-mails, texts, PMs, DMs and whatever other contacts you've had from them. No you don't need the 'nice things they said to you' to cheer you up on a drab Wednesday afternoon. You have yourself, your Spirit, the Universe, your angels and your guides as well as your terrestrial besties for that.

+ Actually do the two things above. Yeah, really. Properly. Yes, even that account. Yes even the slip of paper you keep in your drawer with their number on, just in case. Don't worry if there's an emergency, which there won't be; they will find a way to get in touch with you. If *you* have an emergency call the police/fire department/ambulance/your mum – i.e. someone who can actually help you.

+ Fill your life with awesome stuff like hobbies, friends, exercise, great food, dancing, meditating and move through that shit like a champ. The lonely nights will pass and the sadness will fade. We promise. And while you're working on all that, pray for the healing.

Let's face it, we all know that when a relationship of any sort ends, it feels weird and a bit sad so we do the whole sentimental, reminiscing, remember when… for old times' sake, cute sad face text thing to ease us into the transition. We look at old e-mails and photos. We remember the good times. We sometimes try to rekindle what we had, whether in real life (embarrassing emotionally manipulative e-mail or 1 a.m. booty call anyone?) or in our heads (daydreaming about a dreamy couples round-the-world trip that ain't never happening, perhaps?) but we know in truth all we're doing is dragging out the process. We know in our hearts if it's going anywhere or not.

But we have this sadistic preference for pulling the Band Aid off slowly, slowly over several weeks and months instead of just whipping it off in a split second and being done with it.

It's not the pain of the Band Aid coming off, it's the fear of it no longer being there.

So stop putting yourself through unnecessary pain and treat yourself with the same love, respect and care that you'd advise your BFF to nourish herself with.

The hardest word

Now here's a universal truth if we ever heard one: it's easier if they apologize. Of course love, forgiveness, letting go and moving on flow so much more easily when we get an apology. But we must learn to move on regardless.

Just because we hurt and we feel like we want, may need an apology, it doesn't mean we're going to get it.

You'll remember that *ACIM* says that we can only take our own inventory? That means that we also can't try to extract, manipulate or guilt-trip an apology from someone else. You both have lessons to learn and a hearty dose of truthful fact may well be in order, but the apology is theirs to give, not yours to take.

A heartfelt sorry makes a lot of headway on the healing path, but a lack of one won't and must not stop you walking that journey. You have to know that you can move through situations where you feel pain, or feel you have been wronged, without the condition of getting an apology first. It's a demonstration to yourself that you are capable, healed and whole, regardless of what others say or do, don't say or don't do. In fact it could be one of the most valuable lessons you ever learn and every damn day is a school day.

Likewise we've already covered the bit about being a proper grown-up and apologizing for times where you might have made a boob or been a bit of a meanie, but it doesn't always mean they'll accept the apology, or want to go out drinking tequila slammers with you again. It's a real sucker punch this one, especially when you've worn your heart on your sleeve and put yourself out there to admit your mistake

And just a wee quick word on making mistakes, getting it wrong, being a bit hasty or making a total hash of life, which we all do from time to time #sigh. The Hebrew origin of the word 'sin' is archery terminology for missing the target. So rather than thinking we, or anyone else for that matter, has 'sinned' – *we know, heavy, duuude!* – we can think instead of simply missing the mark, which is so often what we do, when we do wrong. So after that ill-thought comment, misinterpreted text, grumpy tired argument after a 2 a.m. finish on your side, you need to hustle. This is not meant to belittle the hurt that can follow a mistake, rather to aid the shift in perception that is required to move the guilt if it was you, or the bitterness if it was someone else.

Write a forgiveness list and make it like exhaling a long yogic breath. Get it. All. Out. From the smallest annoyance – the latest nasal tweeny-bopper superstar that drives you crazy on YouTube – to a long-held trauma or grievance – the teacher that told you you'd never amount to anything or the absent parent – to things that seems almost unbearable to comprehend – war, torture, abuse and devastation. And, of course, yourself. Make sure you reserve yourself a place on that list for as long as you need it.

Then check in with it on the regular. Some of these people and situations will go quite quickly, others will stay there for a long time. Cross them off as you do the work. Add them again if you need to. Think of it as your go-to whenever you need some forgiveness action. Feeling bitter and twisted? Pissed off and little bit crazed? Check your list! Or whenever the loving mood strikes you. Pick one of these bad boys off and see them or it through the eyes of the Universe – as perfect, whole and innocent – and send some killer loving vibes.

Remember forgiveness is not about letting them off the hook; it's about letting you off the hook.

Like a magical addition to your energy management routine, forgiveness is not only a guaranteed fast track to making miracles and releasing dead emotional weight, it's also a really important part of curating a high-vibe life. From taking a breath and smiling when someone barges you out of the way to get on the train first, to taking a breath and thinking of your partner as an innocent child and remembering all the ways you love them, after an argument.

Forgiveness doesn't mean being walked all over; sometimes the most loving answer is no. But sometimes for the sake of your own energy it's more kind, generous and productive for both off you if you can see the situation for what it is; two or more egos playing together to keep you all small and get you stuck on the downward spiral all day long, when all your Spirit wants to do is paaarrr-tay!

SPIRITUAL SMACKDOWN: YOU'VE HURT PEOPLE TOO

Unless you are a ratified saint you too have most likely hurt and offended people, sniggered behind their backs sharing screen grabs on WhatsApp or bitched about their outfit. You may have even, and we're just saying maybe, been dishonest, cheated, stolen, double-crossed, back-stabbed, bullied, been two-faced, manipulative and/or judgemental at some point in your life. Just saying, maybe.

And if you recognize any of those behaviours from your past, or your present, we're sure you'll understand how important it is to remember those times when you've 'missed the mark' and become the one hoping for forgiveness.

Remember that movie, *Pay It Forward*? If you're under 30 that is probably a resounding no, so you should go watch it. For those of you who haven't seen it, the premise is that this class of little kids gets a school assignment to come up with an idea that could change the world. This one kid comes up with the idea that if every person 'paid forward' (instead of paid back… clever huh?!) a good deed to three other people, then the world would become an exponentially more incredible place, at warp speed.

You need to think of forgiveness and humility like this. Someone may have wronged you, hurt you, lied to you. But you too have hurt people in the past. Maybe they forgave you, maybe they didn't. But either way you would have wanted to be forgiven. So pay that forward. Don't be the missing link in the chain that stops the good vibes flowing because your high-school friend never forgave you for stealing her boyfriend.

Or we could get even more old school on you than a movie reference from Y2K and paraphrase the Bible: let those without sin cast the first stone.

Unless you're perfect, holy and enlightened, and have been since birth, not a single day off, you have some love to pay forward, some humility to spare and maybe even a little grace in the bank for when a brother or sister goes off track. And if you are enlightened, of course, you don't need us to tell you that ;-)

IF ONLY I COULD TURN BACK TIME: GUILT AND REGRET

In this modern world where we can spend so much time in our heads, comparing and judging ourselves from within, without much respite, it can be difficult to believe you are the most important person on your forgiveness hit list. Guilt and regret can make forgiving ourselves feel out of reach and like an almost alien concept.

There is a really good chance that you might even be twitching to skip this chapter altogether and we empathize – when we sat down to write this particularly difficult discourse we too felt some resistance to start tapping away at the MacBook, as it speaks to the most tender, sore and emotional parts of our human existence.

If you're nodding along to that you are not alone. So many of us relate to the burden of guilt and regret despite the perfect smiles we post on our social media apps. Which is exactly why we wanted to go deep on these ickiest of topics known to (hu) man to help you delve into those dark, shadowy depths and understand what we can learn, how we can move on and heal.

A title like this one can make even the most able unicorn rider start to feel a knot in their stomach, but please stick with us. Boo. Guilt and regret are like evil twins that hold us back from truly embracing our #HigherSelfie, no matter where we are on our spiritual journey today.

For many of us *guilt* is the feeling of being in the wrong because we couldn't or wouldn't make an authentic choice for ourselves, often because of battling the pressure of keeping up appearances, busy-ness or exhaustion, which we accept as our default.

And *regret* is just a fancy word the ego made up for wasting time thinking about stuff you did or didn't do in the past, which as we all know by now, doesn't exist anyhoo.

Yet we're willing to bet that way back even Buddha had a few grizzly flashbacks, so against that backdrop be kind to yourself as we walk this together and feel everything you need to.

Cringe. Shudder. Gulp. OK, let's go there...

We can all look back at scenarios from our past and shiver at what we did, said and saw, or chose not to at the time, or perhaps what someone or something did to us.

What makes guilt and regret so slippery is that they have the ability to creep up and ambush us when we're triggered by the world around us. It might be a song coming on the radio that reminds you of 'that night', catching the eye of someone across a room and seeing they are still embarrassed by the DM you ignored, smelling the fragrance you used to wear that bubbles up the conversation you should have had or scrolling Facebook and seeing a passive-aggressive comment aimed at you.

> Spirit will send you signs that it's time to 'hold the stare' with even the grimmest of feelings because there's healing work to do in this lifetime – and the pangs of guilt and yearning of regret are holding you back.

It's really easy to push awkward memories to the back of our minds and it's super-easy to distract ourselves with the rush of modern life – gym workouts, pub binges, marathon Tinder dating schedules – but by avoiding the awks we are destined to bump into these ghosts over and over as they stop us from being in the present, at peace and feeling full of love in our relationships.

You are not your deeds, actions or words and to access life more on the #HigherSelfie level that you deserve, and you *do* deserve it, you must acknowledge and move on to break the energetic hangover of your past.

For the time you went too far, too fast. When you cheated on that guy, lied to your friend, stole money or copied work and took the credit for it. When you settled for an answer you knew wasn't right. When you cast a blind eye and turned your back or when you couldn't protect yourself because you were too young to know what was happening. For the grudges you bear, the jealousy and the sabotage. For letting them drift away. For making them stay. For all of the guilt you have taken on and the regret about what you did or didn't do, whatever your perception of the relationship or experience that hangs heavy in your heart, you must switch to a new intention and allow yourself to heal.

Lucy: Lose what doesn't serve you

After a particularly messy and emotional break-up (as if there is any other kind?!), rather than acknowledging my feelings and looking after myself, I ended up partying pretty hard. I started going out a lot and enjoying all the trappings of the club scene and totally lost any sense of the self-worth and discernment I had before.

I made a lot of dodgy choices that I lived to regret and while I can look back and see it as a bad period, the sort many people can relate to, the memories of it still make me shudder when they return as flashbacks today. The guilt I felt about those poor choices has been hard to budge but I'm committed to accepting it as part of my own journey. It's a case of let go or be dragged down – and those funky feelings just don't serve me.

Let that shit go

Living in the past, reworking it, over-analysing what happened and replaying the words you could have spoken or wish you'd taken back, will exhaust you, squash your spirit and keep you holding on to something that doesn't actually exist. Can you say exhausting?!

There is no mistake in the Universe so whatever you're regretting was meant to happen exactly as it did to show you the way to where you are now. But what do we do about it when we're actually feeling it and trying to hold back the tears that accompany it?

A little spiritual theory is helpful here. *ACIM* teaches that there is you, y'know, the real you that knows the truth of your awesomeness and your divine connection to the Universe and all that jazz, then there's the Holy Spirit, who straddles the human world and the heavens.

The Holy Spirit sees your pain but doesn't buy in to it with you – like all good BFFs!

The Holy Spirit is like the operator that connects you on your hotline to the divine. Then there is God (we're using the G-word here because *ACIM* does, but switch it up if you'd prefer) who only sees your perfection. God does not see your mistakes, your fears, where you have done wrong and made yourself guilty. God only sees you in the perfection in which you were created, no matter what has passed in your life.

So if the divine creator of the entire Universe cannot see your guilt, it's kind of arrogant to think that you have the power and wisdom to override that vision and lay your own judgement on your situation. You're invited to join in with all that love and acceptance and give yourself the grace and compassion that is your divine right. As Brené Brown says, 'You are imperfect, you are wired for struggle, but you are worthy of love and belonging.'

Ultimately, guilt is the ego's prison for us. If you're wandering around perpetually feeling guilty, or making others guilty, then you're stuck right where ego wants you – it's time to release yourself. The Universe handed you a get-out-of-jail-free card the minute you were born, to deploy whenever your ego has you behind bars.

Calling time on the blame game

There's a reason that the tit-for-tat nature of back-and-forth bickering is called 'the blame game' – that's because, like a morose match of tennis, you fall into the trap of blaming and it gets passed to and fro like a racquet sport rally (the only difference being you're probably *not* wearing your white micro skirt) but goes something like this:

'Well I reacted like this because you…'

'But you upset me first because…'

'Yeah and you knew I was having a bad day because of…'

'Well it's not my fault that you hate your job…'

'Maybe if you were more supportive…'

And on and on, stuck forever in a game of emotional one-upmanship. At some point someone will feel guilty enough and give in, or get tired of the argument, storm out and pop that one in their back pocket for the rematch, which will invariably escalate: 'Well it got so bad that I had to leave the room…'

So we can see that feeling guilty and trying to manipulate others from a place of guilt doesn't work. A little guilt itch can, however, be just the push you need to sort your life out – we can use this power for good!

Brené Brown says that guilt can be motivating in positive ways. Guilt feels utterly gross, but if it makes you apologize and clean up the physical mess you made (hands up, who's not perfect either?!) that's good. And if it makes you think twice before you say or do the same thing again, even better. That's just part of growing up and being a responsible adult.

Carrying guilt around like a stick to beat yourself with helps no one. So it's crucial to clean that mess up – inside and out – and move on knowing you did your best to fix it.

Taking inventory

It's contagious. When you make yourself guilty, you make others guilty, perhaps without even realizing.

The Universal cosmic law says 'as within, so without'. The Bible says 'do unto others as you would have them do to you.' They both mean the same thing: if you're failing to love yourself, you're failing to love others. If you believe in your own guilt, you also believe in theirs. If you're judging yourself, you're probably judging them too.

The thing is it's nigh impossible to feel guilt and not lay it on others. And by guilt we're talking wider context stuff as well as the obvious kind of guilt here – judging yourself and comparing yourself are all forms of guilt. You're guilty of not being thin enough, cool enough, rich enough, or just enough, of anything.

Notice what you notice. If you're holding yourself to those standards you are almost certainly holding other people in your life to those standards too, whether you're nagging, bitching, or whining to their face or just keeping it all inside.

The more you judge, compare and guilt-trip other people, the more judged and guilty you will feel yourself, even if no one is projecting that back at you. But who'd blame them if they were?

The past is over

This calls for some serious spiritual activism. You can officially let go of everything that happened before and stop letting it define the way you see yourself and others now.

You can stop holding your friends/partner/parents/workmates to the mistakes, real or perceived, they have made in the past, forgive and move forwards.

You may regret some of your health choices to date but guess what? You get to choose again!

It may have been pretty shitty that you forced your partner to make a decision they didn't want to but guess what? You get to choose again!

Perhaps it was a crazy idea to say 'yes' to that job but guess what? You get to choose again!

What a strong person you had to be because your mum walked out on you and your anger has protected you up to now but maybe, for your own sake, it's time to choose again.

Look at the ghosts of your past, write them all down on paper and burn through that emotional baggage with the intention to heal, be free and choose again. By acknowledging the pain of guilt and regret there is room to grow. You get to create your life one choice at a time, from the ground up.

Vulnerability = strength

Luckily there is a fail-safe way to melt those crummy guilty feelings in all their guises, but it's not what you might think, and at first glance it can seem like it would be totally ineffectual while also being a wee bit scary!

The one thing that will stop all kinds of anxiety-inducing, energy-sapping and antiperspirant-testing guilt in its tracks, is vulnerability.

Just like surrender, vulnerability has a different meaning *in here*, than it does *out there*. In spiritual woo-woo land – which is where we really live, obvs – vulnerability is true strength and where your safety lies.

In the outside world vulnerability means being open to hurt and pain. In fact a quick online search throws up this definition:

*Vulnerable: exposed to the possibility
of being attacked or harmed, either
physically or emotionally.*

*Synonyms: in danger, in peril, in jeopardy,
at risk, endangered, unsafe, unprotected,
ill-protected, unguarded; open to attack,
attackable, assailable, exposed, wide
open; undefended, unshielded, unfortified,
unarmed, without arms, without weapons,
defenceless, easily hurt/wounded/
damaged, powerless, helpless.*

Danger, peril, risk, unsafe, powerless, helpless… Yowzer! No wonder we don't want to feel or be vulnerable. But the truth is that we are open to attack, from others, or ourselves, whether we are consciously vulnerable or not.

The difference is, that when we choose vulnerability the attacks don't stick like they do when we choose to be defensive, and they don't perpetuate.

Defence is a form of attack

Whenever you are defending yourself you are actually attacking, and if there's someone else involved, whether they started it or are coming back at you, they are also attacking. So without vulnerability – the willingness to release defensiveness – we create a battle. And we don't know about you, but we're cool without another battle!

When we choose to be vulnerable we call in and make space for innovation, creativity and change; as the work of our girl Brené Brown preaches, vulnerability is the necessary state to create connection and hand over the crippling weight of trying to stop criticism and offence. You have the choice today, right here, right now to take the lessons of previous experiences, partner these with a heap of good intention and open-hearted effort to be your #HigherSelfie, and leave guilt and regret in the energetic trash.

You can't fake it so don't bother

Another awesome side effect of vulnerability is that it massively ups your ability to be authentic – it is *the* way to show the Universe and other Earthlings that you are 'all in' and ready to be in your truth – whether you're texting that hot guy first or telling your boss you need some help with the project you confidently said you could handle all on your lonesome.

But let's keep the energy clean when we move forwards and always act from the heart. There's no point getting off the hook of guilt and hopping onto the spike of obligation.

For example, paying someone a compliment or trying to do them a favour out of a place of obligation or feeling that you owe them something will only put your ego back in charge, but this time it will be dressed up in one of its fave outfits: 'Holier than thou'.

When you know better, you do better

Your atonement can and should be a moving prayer.

You don't need to spend your days continually judging yourself because judgement has already been passed. As far as the Big U is concerned you are already perfect. (Yay!)

If there is one golden theme that runs through this book it's that our intention and energy is everything. Natch, we're huge advocates of action, but it has to be action from the right place, with the right vibes. From the heart and soul, with love and a desire only for the highest good.

We can change our beliefs by changing our track record when it comes to how we show up in our own lives. As we can only affect change in the present and the present almost immediately becomes the past we have the opportunity in every moment to begin creating a new story for ourselves.

One of the best and most effective ways to change the beliefs you have about yourself, and to build a new track record for a more authentic and aligned you, is with small consistent steps.

So if you want to be the person that takes care of her friends, every single gesture that is aligned with that is a tick on your new track record whether it's being her shoulder to cry on and passing the tissues and ice cream after a break-up or helping her set up her blog with your whizzy web skills. It all delivers on your intention to take care of your gals and *be* the BFF you aspire to be.

If you want to work your way to full yogi status because of the mind, body, soul benefits you feel in your flow, then every bedroom *vinyasa* because you can't make class tonight, is another confident vote for your intention to practise your commitment to yourself.

With authentic intention fuelling your actions, there is very little room for regret and guilt.

SPIRITUAL SMACKDOWN: IT REALLY IS THAT SIMPLE

As we said earlier, we seem to like to make things more complicated than they actually are because then we have a legit excuse for not doing them. In fact it's a very human trait to overcomplicate stuff (and yes, Virgo dudes and babes, you have it even tougher than the rest of us on this one!) so much that perfectly reasonable, simple and helpful-if-only-you-would-start-the-damn-thing tasks become totally unreasonable, why-even-bother-pointless pursuits.

Why are the simplest things always the hardest to start? Why, when we want to get fit, would we rather start a complex regime of underwater yoga and trapeze work that requires a ton of special gear, an intensive training programme and small bank loan, than just getting our kicks on and going for a jog straight out the front door, or working up a sweat dancing to '90s classics in our bedroom?

It's because our fear of failure is so great that we're lining up our excuses before we even begin. It's because we think our 'problems' are so complicated and difficult to unravel that something simple, easy, cheap and joyful couldn't possibly be the answer. And at an even more twisted level it's because our fear of success is even greater than our fear of failure. What if you really did achieve that smokin' hot body you've always wanted? However you do it – whether it's by drinking liquidized spinach and walking a high wire or cutting out Friday night beers and shakin' your groove thang every time the mood strikes you – are you really ready for the result you truly desire?

Are you really ready for that? Are you ready to get out of your (un)comfort zone and experience health, fitness and energy on a whole new level? Are you ready to show yourself that you can change? You can achieve your dreams? And it doesn't need to be complicated, drawn out and expensive?

If we make things harder than they need to be, we convince ourselves – at least on a surface level – and others, that we gave it our best shot, but it just wasn't meant to be. Then we can con ourselves that staying where we are, where we know we don't truly want to be, is the best decision for now. Maybe we'll try again next year.

Jo: If only...

. . . .

How many times have I heard 'If only I had time to meditate' and then seen said person evidently spending hours on Facebook or talking about binge-watching *Game of Thrones?* Awareness is everything. Take a fearless inventory of how you're spending your life and energy and see how easy it would be to shoehorn some simple transformative habits into your day. No. Excuses!

If you believe it's too good to be true, well that's just another sophisticated ego trick. Don't believe five minutes of meditation a day could transform your life? Or eating a vegetarian meal once a day could make you feel lighter and healthier? Just try it. What have you got to lose? In the grand scheme of the amount of time and effort you've lost down the rabbit hole of social media, Netflix and elaborate schemes doomed to fail right from the start because that's how your ego designed them, the answer is really, nothing.

> Hey, if you actually give the simple stuff a
> chance you might even surprise yourself
> – and scare your ego half to death!

IN THE NAME OF LOVE

It's the last chapter so we're going balls out, boys and girls! If we were pushed for an answer to the question of the meaning of life, we'd take a stab at 'love'.

Love is the beginning and love is the end.

Love is the key to spiritual activism and can fuel change in our wider world but starts in our own hearts and homes.

ACIM teaches that only love is real, everything else is an illusion. Everything else is created by the conditions, exceptions, perceptions and misinterpretations that we lay on top of love. But love still remains as the eternal truth. It is our purpose, our journey and what we ultimately return to.

Every great human endeavour has been achieved in the name of true love, whether it's love for a cause, love for another or love for the self.

There is always space for more love in any situation. The love of the Universe is infinitely abundant, therefore the stores of love available to you in any given moment are infinite. All you have to do to access that love, is choose it.

Choose love over fear, over guilt, over shame, over hate, over bitterness, over comparison, over judgement.

There is an old joke, 'How do you make a statue of an elephant?' Answer, 'You just get a block of marble and carve away everything that doesn't look like an elephant!'

We hope you use this book as a guide to carving away everything in your life that doesn't look like love. Every lesson we learn, every time we forgive, every time we grow, every little inch more present and conscious we become, the more love we reveal and the more open our psychic floodgates for love become.

There is a cosmic alarm clock going off around the world. We need you lit up, and aware of your nature as a perfect and whole channel for love and light on Earth. We need you awake, active, alive and full of the knowledge of your own divine greatness, no matter where you come from, what your day job is or how spiritual you and everyone else thinks you may or may not be.

The ego may ask, 'How did the impossible occur? To what did the impossible happen?' and may ask in many forms. Yet there is no answer, only an experience. Seek only this, and don't let theology delay you.

ACIM teaches us that however incomprehensible it may seem only love is real, that love is infinite and you are worthy of all the love of the Universe. Not to be hindered by the ego's questions. Not to try to 'make sense' of it. Not to hold back on love, while you wait for a good enough answer, before you allow it to flow to you and through you.

> Instead, go directly for the experience, and
> know love irrefutably to wake up your life,
> free your soul and find your tribe.

ABOUT THE AUTHORS

Sophia Spring

Lucy Sheridan, AKA The UK's first and only Comparison Coach, is on a mission to get Gen Y over the 'compare & despair' of social media and be truly happy off and online. She has been featured in *Grazia*, *Stella Magazine* and the *Daily Mail* as part of her #comparisonfree campaign, and continues to deliver that message via one-on-one coaching, workshops and speaking gigs. **www.proofcoaching.com**

Jo Westwood, AKA 'The Spirit DJ', remixes ethereal, deep spiritual concepts to make them accessible, practical and relatable. She helps members of the digital generation to be more present, peaceful and connected in this manic modern world so they can fulfill their highest potential in their career and relationships. In short, she delivers spiritual solutions for your real life shiz. **www.jowestwood.com**

Lucy and Jo are co-creators of #HigherSelfie, the spiritual lifestyle brand and home to the world's only spirituality unconference.

f higherselfieco

🐦 #higherselfieco

📷 @higherselfieco

www.higherselfie.co

Notes

Notes

Notes

Notes

Notes

Notes

HAY HOUSE

Look within

Join the conversation about latest products, events, exclusive offers and more.

f Hay House UK

🐦 @HayHouseUK

📷 @hayhouseuk

🖤 healyourlife.com

We'd love to hear from you!

CPSIA information can be obtained
at www.ICGtesting.com
Printed in the USA
FSOW02n1852050316
17644FS